Introduction to Two-Dimensional Design

Introduction to
Two-Dimensional Design:

Understanding
Form and Function

John Bowers

John Wiley & Sons, Inc.
New York, Chichester, Weinheim, Brisbane, Singapore, Toronto

This book is printed on acid-free paper. ∞

Copyright © 1999 by John Wiley & Sons. All rights reserved.

Published simultaneously in Canada.

This publication is designed to provide accurate and authoritative information in regard to the subject matter covered. It is sold with the understanding that the publisher is not engaged in rendering professional services. If professional advice or other expert assistance is required, the services of a competent professional person should be sought.

Library of Congress Cataloging-in-Publication Data:
Bowers, John, 1959–
    Introduction to two-dimensional design : understanding form and
    function / John Bowers.
        p.   cm.
    Published simultaneously in Canada.
    Includes bibliographical references and index.
    ISBN 0-471-29224-9 (pbk. : alk. paper)
    1. Design.   I. Title.
NC703.B68   1998
760—dc21   98-29590
                                                                    CIP

Printed in the United States of America.

10 9 8

Acknowledgments

I would like to thank my family, friends, colleagues, peer reviewers, and all of my many students for their help and support in making this book possible. Special thanks to the American University Aspen Group. Thanks to the Oregon State University Office of Research, and Office of Academic Affairs for their support. Thanks to those who supplied me with work and/or allowed me to use examples of their work. Thanks to Joseph Ansell, School of the Museum of Fine Arts, Boston, Kate Battles, Johnson County Community College, Jorge Frascara, University of Alberta, Edmonton, and Jeff Jensen, Western Kentucky University for their critique of the manuscript, and Karin C. Warren for her help in organization and editing.

Thanks to my mother, Betty McMurry, Ed.S. and sister Susan Bowers, Ph.D., for their research assistance in a number of cognition-related issues and help in editing. Special thanks to my wife, Helene, for her patience and assistance, and Hu Hung Shu for his guidance and his family for their generosity. This book is dedicated to my parents for their continual support and insight.

Contents

Introduction

Underlying Ideology

This book was written to help you more fully understand and participate in the world around you. I hope it will further your knowledge and ability as you experience, create, interpret and critique forms and their messages, and that it will prepare you for additional explorations in design. Above all, I hope it will help you better understand your experiences and interests, and enhance your abilities in all areas of study and activity, espe-cially the ability to question. To a large degree, the principles, methods, and issues discussed transcend visual form.

This book's discussions are based on my experiences, research, professional practice, and teaching in the field of design. While many of its concepts are basic to design, I have sought to extend them by presenting a broad, current perspective on the role of design as a discipline of study that can lead to any num-ber of activities and outcomes.

It is my goal to demonstrate and explain how form organizes and shapes (and is shaped by) the function, context meaning, and interpretation of ideas and concepts. These terms are described later in this introduction.

To accomplish this goal, the book focuses on the human-made environment. It identifies and describes visual components and principles specific to two-dimensional design. It explains how our understanding of these principles has evolved, the impor-tant theories and methods of creating and evaluating their use, and the issues related to the way we interact as a people through form. Finally, it demonstrates how form and its inter-pretation have helped shape our environment and, conversely, how environment has shaped form.

It is not my intent to provide a selected view of visual form based on personal likes and dislikes and to critique in terms of good and bad. Instead, I explain the selected forms and evaluate them according to criteria that examine appearances as a way of creating meaning.

Aesthetics, or the study of beauty, is not a focus of this book. While a form can inspire us through its beauty or may be part of a marketing strategy, it has many more functions that include helping us understand ourselves and others.

This book is based on the belief that an understanding of form is possible and important. Understanding the relationships among elements and the methods that create form can help you better visualize and make sense of the images you see, use, or create.

This book seeks to present a balance between the objective and the subjective and a basis for deciding when to employ each. Form and its function should not be created and understood solely through a single method or theory. Several important and at times competing methods and theories are addressed, all which should be considered. Methods based on intuition, play, and chance, along with empirical research, can be used alone or in combination.

This book can be a course supplement or a stand-alone reader. It is not meant as a manual to be strictly followed or applied without consideration to context. As a reference guide, it is suitable for students in any discipline and for those outside academia because it seeks to relate learning from many disciplines. The chapters can be read in any order. However, it might be helpful to start at the beginning, where many terms are defined.

About the Images and Their Use

The images in this book were chosen to help you realize that design is already a part of your life. You not only view form and interpret messages in your everyday life but also create both through your actions. For example, what you purchase or how you vote result in the creation (or elimination) and understanding of objects and methods of interaction.

0-1
**Facade of the Miriam Wosk Residence, 1984
Beverly Hills, California**
Frank Gehry and Associates

Accompanying the discussion in each chapter are design examples by highly recognized individuals or those in collaboration as well as those less known and some without formal education. The variety of images demonstrates the broad nature of design problems and solutions.

This book does not seek to polarize fine art and applied design activities but to find their commonalities. It addresses activities or concerns that are personal in nature (yet may be shared by a wide segment of the population) and that may originate primarily from the self; at the same time, it focuses on activity that undertakes communication beyond personal expression or that which is disseminated on a large scale.

This book focuses on two-dimensional design to narrow the breadth of a discussion that examines both form and its implications. However, because we live in a multidimensional world, I have included some examples of three- and four-dimensional work (video and film). These examples exhibit a strong two-dimensional presence when viewed from a particular angle (figure 0-1), or their creation was contingent on the two-dimensional display of their underlying concepts or structure.

Some works are referred to more than once. This is done to demonstrate specific principles or issues as well as to show that any single work can be analyzed in a number of ways to examine its various aspects and meanings.

At any time throughout history form has been influenced by the past. The concerns, styles, and even whole images of earlier works have been appropriated or served as objects against which subsequent designers work. This is noted when particularly pertinent.

0-2
**Symbol for American
Foundation for AIDS
Research, 1987**
Dan Friedman

This work encompasses many
of the concepts used throughout this book.

Concepts and Terms

The following concepts and terms are discussed and used extensively in this book and later described in more detail. While these underlie many discussions of form, the following definitions apply primarily only to the context of this book.

Design

Design is commonly defined as the arrangement of visual elements that underlie the making of form in the fine arts and applied design disciplines. But design is also the methods, theory, and research that form-making is based upon. These examine the use and implications of form and the role form plays in shaping culture (beliefs, goals, rituals, language and history shared or grouped among a people). In this sense, design is a process of inquiry, a means of understanding and a way of guiding interaction, as much as a signifier of physical forms.

Form

Form is the result of human or natural activity. It may be visual or, in a broader sense, it may be a method that leads to a visual outcome. The symbol in figure 0-2 has a clearly defined form: it is square and made up several color areas over which is a grouping of unified letters.

Function

Function refers to a form's practical, spiritual, cultural, or personal use. While function is generally a component of three-dimensional design professions, such as industrial design and architecture, it also plays a role in two-dimensional design, where *function* is synonymous with *purpose,* with a form's intent. This includes an evaluation of why the form was created, its audience, how it will be used, and what it will do (persuade, enlighten, or inform). For example, the AIDS symbol has the primary function of serving as an identifiable marking for an event.

Meaning

Meaning is the message and use of a form, both symbolic and literal. This book emphasizes meaning and explores the many layers of meaning a form can evoke.

Interpretation

Interpretation is the translation of a form's meaning, or layers of meaning, through the filter of different perspectives. Viewpoint is based on experiences and needs. It may flow from a range of philosophical ideologies from feminism to Marxism, however consciously or unconsciously applied.

Rather than giving factual information about a form's color interactions, for example, an interpretation attempts to define its meaning and to explain how the color interactions affect us.

Ambiguity

A form is ambiguous when it has two or more possible meanings or interpretations. Ambiguity can be accompanied by contradiction, which has seemingly conflicting points of view or competing form and function. Ambiguity and contradiction should be accepted in both the design of a work and in its interpretation. The appropriateness of each can only be determined by the specific circumstances.

The AIDS symbol in figure 0-2 is relatively unambiguous, although one might interpret the meaning of the three backgrounds differently. It also has a single message to convey: an event to support research into AIDS.

Appropriateness

Appropriateness is the suitability of a form—for example, whether it is right or wrong for a particular purpose. Appropriateness is a subjective determination made through experience, regulation, research, and a knowledge of the intended audience and cultural environment in which the form will be placed.

CHAPTER 1 | Definitions, Sources, and Roles

Understanding Design as a Discipline

About This Chapter

This chapter discusses how we are viewers, users, and designers of form. It examines design and form as well as how design influences and is influenced by culture.

Concepts and Terms in This Chapter

Design

Form

Function

Meaning

Convention

Evaluation

Roles

1-1 (Previous page and above)
Sign at Gas Station
Portland, Oregon

The many forms and functions of two-dimensional design are all around us. They originate from a variety of needs, serve many purposes, and portray a wide range of information, ideas, and concerns.

Defining Design

Thinking Broadly

The word *design* is both a noun and a verb—that is, it signifies a product of thinking and an extension of thinking. The word has its roots in the Italian verb *disegnare,* which means to create. Whether understood as a noun or a verb or both, design is all around us: in human-made and natural forms, and in the ways we communicate and understand one another and our environment.

Design becomes tangible through visual elements, principles of organization, and methods of creating and evaluating form. These components of design activity are not unlike those that govern other communications disciplines, such as language. By becoming familiar and fluent with these components, you can better produce and interpret messages. Unlike language, however, visual components need not necessarily adhere to a logical set of rules that are easily transferable among design problems.

Design is, in part, the visual appearance of forms that result from the use of components—but a more critical definition considers the many other aspects of form. It embraces the meaning and interpretation of form and the issues form addresses. These issues might include how to direct others through a public space or ways to build understanding among diverse groups.

As outlined in the Introduction, this book defines design in the broadest possible context, treating it as both a noun and a verb. Through this definition, the book examines the qualitative (subjective, perhaps intuitive) aspects of design and the quantitative (objective, perhaps rational) aspects. When used together, these aspects can create meaningful and engaging form.

Design as a Discipline of Study

"The most important ideas in design can be found in the spaces between the disciplines."[1]

American Center for Design

Design is a discipline or subject of study that engages not only in visual explorations but also in those cultural, social, and philosophical in nature. In this sense, design encompasses, but is more than, the technical and business aspects of applied activities common to architecture, landscape, and interior architecture; industrial design; graphic design; and a number of hybrid professions.

"To me design . . . is a way of discussing life."[2]

Ettore Sottsass, Jr.

Because the methods of creating and evaluating design are largely based on models and learning from other disciplines, design is inherently cross-disciplinary. Two-dimensional design, particularly graphic design, draws directly on studies in anthropology, communications, education, history, psychology, and sociology. For example, psychological studies into how we perceive and understand messages may inform the design of forms to be used by people of diverse backgrounds (figure 1-2). Designing also draws more abstractly on disciplines that foster the creative spirit, such as literature, music and philosophy. These help us understand, confront, or express the many mysteries of life.

The forms that result from design activity and the methods of creating and evaluating form are, in turn, an aid to learning in other disciplines. The problem-solving process common in design and a subject of study in psychology (described in chapter 2) has recently been applied in some middle schools to further the understanding of language, arts, mathematics, and social studies.[3]

1-2
Don't Walk Signs
10th and Burnside, Portland, Oregon

The same information can be communicated in a number of ways. The most effective method depends on the audience and context.

The Basis of Design

Satisfying Needs and Addressing Issues

As humans, we have basic, practical needs that must be met to sustain life. At the minimum, we require food, water, and shelter. We also have varying degrees of emotional and personal needs, including the desire to pursue and find meaning, self-fulfillment, and a sense of security.

Design originates from basic human needs and desires. Since early recorded history, humans have sought to coexist with (and at times control) others and the human-made and natural environment (figure 1-3).

While form has its basis in needs, it is influenced by forces that are political, economic, technical, and philosophical in nature. These forces and the issues they generate work either independently or together in some combination to help create the appearance, understanding, and use of form.

As design satisfies needs it is most meaningful when it addresses broader issues that underlie problems and conditions that a solution can seek to express or change. These can be personal issues or those shared by a large segment of society. These may include issues cultural or social in nature, such as creating understanding among diverse groups, or those philosophical, such as ethical decision-making.

1-3
Titris Hoyuk,
Early Turkish Settlement,
2400–2200 B.C.

As illustrated in this recently discovered and earliest known example of urban planning, design can bring us together in meaningful ways.

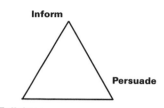

1-4
Relationship of the Primary Functions of Form

Diagrams are useful for simplifying and conveying ideas but are only generalizations of highly complex interactions.

The Purpose of Design

Defining Form and Function

The broad study of design can be narrowed by focusing on form and function and examining the underlying ideologies, needs, purposes, and implications of form. By understanding the function of form, we can better understand how form connects us to each other and to the world.

Form has numerous meanings, some twenty of which are distinguishable. Many of these meanings are derived from the Latin word *forma,* which is based on Greek words for shape, structure, and idea. At the core of these, form is the combination of basic visual elements of size, color, and texture, and is more than shape alone.

Every form has a primary function and many subsidiary ones. Function is obvious in some forms. A saw, for example, has the mechanical function of dividing pieces of wood. In two-dimensional form, function can be more abstract and difficult to define. A painting has no mechanical function but it does serve a purpose in that it can inspire, inform, or move us to action.

In figure 1-4, each of the three functions influences the other and, depending on the problem to be addressed, the triangle might not be equilateral. To inform includes clarifying, explaining, and identifying; to enlighten includes revealing; and to persuade includes suggestion (common in advertising).

1-5
The American Sign Language Alphabet

Two-dimensional form can represent movements and aid in understanding and communicating.

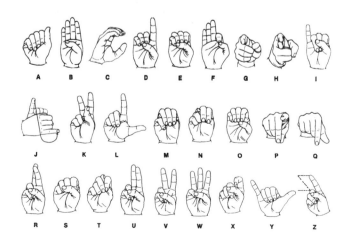

1-6
Portrait of Seated Man, 1965
Alberto Giacometti

Two-dimensional form can
serve more than one function;
the dominant will depend on
our interpretation.

1-7
**Limestone Relief from
the Tomb of Ny-ankh-nesuwt
Egypt, 2400 B.C.**

In perhaps its highest calling
since recorded history, form
can tell us about ourselves
and create understanding.

Balancing Form and Function

"It is not enough to say how beautiful—one must ask why was it done?"[5]

Massimo Vignelli

"Form follows function."[6]
(circa 1852)

Horatio Greenough

"Form follows fiasco."[7]
(circa 1977)

Peter Blake

The relationship between form and function is open to debate as illustrated in this commentary on the validity of the previous time honored quote.

Anthropologists have found that "primitive" cultures rarely created form for visual pleasure alone. This is generally attributed to their preoccupation with survival. While technological advances have allowed us to create form solely for visual pleasure, the relationship of form to its function remains an important consideration.

The beauty of a form, although highly subjective, is an important consideration in the creation or evaluation of form. Aesthetics (a branch of philosophy that examines the nature of sensory perception and the experience and definition of beauty) has an important place in design. Visually pleasing form (and perhaps ugly form) can enlighten and engage us in its message. Depending on the situation, aesthetics might be the primary consideration.

But aesthetics is only one among many considerations in creating expressive and informative form. The adage "form follows function" suggests that a form's visual appearance should serve primarily to transmit information (figure 1-9). Such work is not clouded by decoration or personal interpretation of the content that alters an objective understanding (a highly relative term) of the message.

While an "objective" position may be appropriate in many situations, its use on a wide scale is open to increasing debate. To some, it narrows the possibilities of design because it fails to fully involve the designer and the audience in creating meaning. The interplay between form and function can best be decided in the context of individual problems and their context.

1-8
Markings
A.D. **900–1200**
Newspaper Rock, Arizona

Early drawings aided in the search for meaning, their form and beauty a result of their primary function.

1-9

Page from *SF Access*, 1992
Richard Saul Wurman

The form of this book directly reveals its function: to convey information about the San Francisco area in easily seen groupings.

Noe Valley/Castro/Upper Market

small dinner menu consisting of the soup of the day, green salads, small pizzas, pan-fried trout, steamed mussels, chicken, and desserts is served four nights a week. ◆ Cafe ◆ Cover. Daily; W-Sa dinner. 2170 Market St (between Church and Sanchez Sts). 861.5016

3 Scandinavian Delicatessen/Restaurant ✦$ Plain, homey, and as trusting as they get in a big city, this long-established restaurant works on the honor system. You order whatever you want, remember what you've eaten, and report what it was to the cashier on the way out. Scandinavians have known about this place for years, and now others have discovered it. Favorite Scandinavian salads, fish, meatballs, and pork are always available. It isn't the most sophisticated fare you'll find, but it's like eating in Grandma's kitchen (if Grandma was Scandinavian), and the management's trusting nature just makes you feel good. ◆ Scandinavian ◆ M-F lunch. 2251 Market St (between Sanchez and Noe Sts). 861.9913

4 Cafe Flore $ For coffee, snacks, or just people watching, this is the ultimate Upper Market hangout. Everyone in the city's counterculture seems to end up here eventually, sipping and schmoozing under the corrugated-metal roof. It's a favorite haunt of authors, would-be authors, film buffs, punks, and just about any other bohemian type who wants to be where the action is. ◆ Cafe ◆ Daily. 2298 Market St (at Noe St). 621.8579

5 La Mediterranee ★★★$ It's easy to understand why the owners have succeeded: The food is good—and cheap. The "Mediterranean Meza," made for two or more, gives a pretty good overview of the kitchen by presenting 10 Middle Eastern specialties, all quite wonderful, on a large platter. There is also reasonably priced party catering. ◆ Middle Eastern ◆ Tu-F lunch and dinner; Sa-Su brunch and dinner. 288 Noe St (at Market and 16th Sts). 431.7210. Also at: 2210 Fillmore St (between Sacramento and Clay Sts). 921.2956; 2936 College Ave, Berkeley. 510/540.7773

6 Joseph Schmidt Confections This small shop is where chocoholics go to worship. Joseph Schmidt, who has mastered chocolate sculpture, creates bowls, flowers, sports equipment, animals, bottles, and automobiles in his edible medium. He also makes the best chocolate truffles in town—maybe anywhere. ◆ M-Sa. 3489 16th St (between Church and Sanchez Sts). 861.8682

7 Ixia When daisies just won't do, this unusual florist specializes in exotic, esoteric plants and flowers. ◆ M-Sa. 2331 Market St (between Castro and Noe Sts). 431.3134

8 The Names Project This is the visitor's center for those who create the panels of remembrance that form the AIDS quilt. The quilt has been exhibited around the world to commemorate those who have died of AIDS and to draw attention to the toll the epidemic has taken. ◆ Daily. 2362 Market St (between Castro and Noe Sts). 863.1966. Administrative offices: 310 Townsend St, Suite 310. 882.5500

9 Inn on Castro $$ One of the smaller guesthouses in the city (five rooms, each with private bath), this inn's intimate surroundings make it truly a home away from home. Although located in an Edwardian town house, its interiors are contemporary: white walls, track lighting, classic Modern furniture, brilliant flowers, and the original art of one of the owners. Upstairs, breakfast is served every morning on an extensive and ever-changing collection of imported china and stoneware dishes. ◆ 321 Castro St (at Market St). 861.0321

10 The Randall Museum The emphasis at this nature and history museum is on participation, with live animals and a petting corral, a ceramics room, a woodworking shop, a seismograph, and biology classes. An environmental learning garden is currently under construction. Many special workshops and events are offered, especially during the summer. ◆ Free. Tu-Sa. 199 Museum Way (at Roosevelt Way). 554.9600

11 Twin Peaks Always lively, always friendly, this was the first gay drinking establishment in San Francisco to come out of the closet by having large picture windows where clients could see and be seen. ◆ Daily. 401 Castro St (off Market St). 864.9470

11 The Bead Store All kinds of nifty beads and unique pieces of jewelry are displayed for those who want to do things themselves, or have their adornment done by someone else with lots of talent. ◆ Daily. 417 Castro St (off Market St). 861.7332

11 Bare Necessities You'll find a variety of natural skin-care products here, from herbal deodorant to vegetable-oil soaps from Provence. ◆ Daily. 421 Castro St (off Market St). 621.6206

11 Castro Theatre San Francisco officialdom dubbed this structure the finest example of a 1930s movie palace in the city. Designed by **Pflueger/Miller** in 1922, the 1,600-seat theater has earned its reputation because of its remarkable Spanish colonial architecture. The auditorium ceiling is probably the most noteworthy feature, an extraordinary affair cast in plaster to resemble a giant cloth canopy tent, complete with swags, ropes, and tassels. And in what better setting could you enjoy an ever-changing series of movies from Hollywood's heyday? Anybody who swoons over *Camille* or drools over the exquisite timing in *Bringing Up Baby* will want to take in a flick at this classic theater. ◆ 429 Castro St (off Market St). 621.6120

138

The Nature of Design

Conventions of Form and Understanding

"Even the simplest things are very complicated when you look at them closely."[8]

Henry Petroski

"No national model is exportable."[9]

Andrea Branzi

Much of two-dimensional form is based on conventions. These are accepted ways of doing or understanding things such as driving on the right side of the road (in most countries) and are the result of informal collective agreement or formal legislation. Conventions are based on factors including tradition, social and political forces, technology, common sense, and even chance.

The appearance and use of form can influence culture and our perception of it (figure 1-10). Conventions can reinforce existing stereotypes and overcoming them can be slow and difficult. New knowledge, thinking and presentations are often perceived as a threat to existing order and power.

A common convention occurs in mapping, where north is aligned at the top of the page and east to the right. This orientation, to a large degree is a result of early maps drawn by Ptolemy A.D. 90–160.[10] The better-known places in his world were placed in the upper right corner for more convenient study. There is, however, nothing inherently correct about such an arrangement, which may be interpreted as placing values on certain land masses and cultures (figure 1-11).

1-10
Man Walking, **1887**
Eadweard Muybridge

Relationships hidden to the human eye were revealed through photographs that in turn helped change existing theories of human motion.

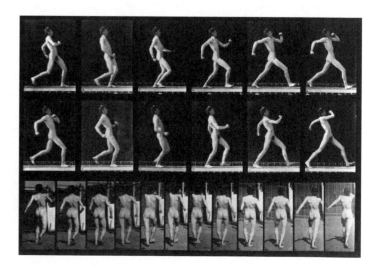

1-11
*A New World of Under-
standing,* **1982**
Jessie Levine

By changing our accepted
method of presentation, we can
alter our understanding of relationships and values.

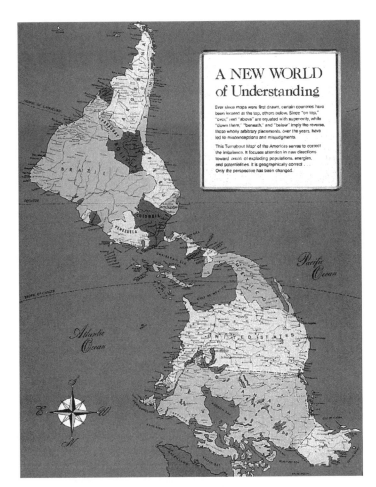

1-12
Corn Palace (1996 Facade)
Mitchell, South Dakota
Cal Schultz, Designer
Dean Strand, Corn Grower

Some design defies convention
by using unexpected materials
(corn, in this instance) in highly
playful ways.

The Meaning of Design

Evaluating Design

As numerous design exhibitions and much discourse have revealed, the question "what is good design?" is not easily answered. Our inclination is to deem a design as "good" according to its appearance, our personal tastes, and the dictates of current trends and styles. Market forces and changing social attitudes also influence our opinions, particularly in clothing and automobile design.

In determining whether or not a design is good, we might better employ our experience, learning, and research (if applicable) to ask whether or not the design works in the context of the situation.

No formula exists to ensure that design fulfills the three primary functions (inform, enlighten, and persuade) yet is also visually pleasing, useful, and meaningful. Adherence to formulas is useful in scientific exploration where results can be objectively evaluated and the aim is to create transferable or reproducible solutions, but in design there is no single correct answer to a given problem.

Good design is often termed inspiring, memorable, useful, and original. These words have multiple meanings and represent concepts that might not be applicable or desirable in all situations.

1-13
Cow Mural
Marathon County, Wisconsin
Designer Unknown

Vernacular design (work generally done by those without formal training and/or distinctive to a particular region) often has a spontaneity, originality, and honesty that may be lacking in so-called good design.

The Role of the Designer

Designer as Interpreter and Mediator

"If my voice comes through in the work and a client sees it as the fulfillment of a need for them, then I have achieved the best possible solution. What I am striving to produce is design that satisfies both my needs and my client's."[13]

Lucille Tenazas

"To be successful, designers must appreciate and reconcile multiple viewpoints about the same topic."[14]

Meredith Davis and Robin Moore

While designers primarily serve as transmitters of messages, roles increasingly assumed throughout the twentieth century are those of interpreters and mediators. These latter roles are needed for balancing the competing needs of the audience, the client (if one is involved) and other voices that may influence work. As you create messages and participate in their dissemination, one or all of the roles may be assumed.

Designers are more than makers, observers, or controllers of information and ideas. At their best, designers are participants in the creation, critique, and dissemination of culture. In this sense their role may be other than the hero-figure (one who provides a single-minded vision, as popularized in the media), to one who has an intimate understanding and empathy for the uniqueness of situations.

To be an interpreter is to take an active role in the issues you choose to address, and their presentation rather than simply transmit messages created by others without regard to their consequence. This may require assuming the role of a mediator: balancing personal needs, the needs of the client (if involved) and audience through the examination of issues from a range of disciplines.

To move beyond mere transmission requires empathy for others, an ability to balance conflicting points of view, and a thorough understanding of the problem and issues at hand, the audience and purpose. The extent to which one assumes these roles should be influenced by the context of the work. The resulting benefit of assuming both roles for the designer is empowerment and increased contribution. The audience benefits by more fully experiencing a designer's insight and learning.

CHAPTER 2 | Research, Theory, and Methods

Understanding and Shaping Response

About This Chapter

This chapter examines how research, theory, and methods of creating and evaluating form play a role in design.

Concepts and Terms in This Chapter

Research

Theory

Method

Intuition

Gestalt Theory

Semiotic Theory

Information Theory

Methodology

Problem-Solving

Diagramming

2-1 (Previous page and above)
**Public Information
Symbols, 1974**
Roger Cook and Don Shanosky

Visual form can inform and
direct us.

16

Defining Research, Theory, and Methods

Balancing the Quantitative and Qualitative

While design is primarily qualitative in nature, it may also include aspects that are quantitative. Both qualitative and quantitative activities can play a significant role in revealing issues and connections in the creation, evaluation, and understanding of form and their messages.

Quantitative design work entails investigation and research. Research requires a designated plan based on a clear statement of the problem from which the search for answers proceeds. At the foundation of research lie theories that aid understanding and direct investigations. Theories are in turn organized and tested through methodologies that, in design, take many forms. Some methodologies such as problem-solving (to be discussed later in this chapter) progress in a methodical, if not linear manner.

But not all two-dimensional design work is based on clearly defined and observable methods akin to those used in the sciences. Work on the design of a poster, for instance, may rely more on qualitative methods: intuition and experience, simple common sense, or sudden inspiration.

American designer Paul Rand (1914–1996) understood intuition as a flash of insight and asserted that most good ideas in the field of communication take shape through intuition.[1] The extent to which this is true, as with the usefulness of more objective methods, depends on the situation at hand. Design as an activity is similar to many disciplines in the humanities in that different methods can be chosen to solve the same problem and result in very different yet appropriate solutions.

The Role of Research in Design

Types of Research and Their Purpose

Research helps us understand and interpret our natural and human-made environment. Its general purpose is to search for and create new information, clarify relationships or bodies of accepted knowledge, and critically interpret existing information. Research often raises as many new questions as it attempts to answer.

Two-dimensional form is heavily influenced by research in the discipline of psychology as well as those of anthropology, sociology, and philosophy. These disciplines investigate human cognition, communication, and culture. The symbols commonly used to direct activity in public spaces (figure 2-1) were developed using psychological and sociological research, which included studies on how information is processed by people from different cultural backgrounds and on how we perceive symbols at varying distances and under varying conditions.

Applied design activity, such as graphic design (where the results generally have a specific audience, are disseminated widely, and seek a specific response), can employ the research methods or results of research from other disciplines. During World War II, for example, designers developed camouflage (figure 2-2) based on research by psychologists into how the human eye perceives form.

2-2
HMS Montezuma, 1942

Research determined the most effective patterning for camouflage for British war ships in World War II.

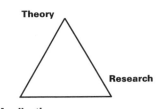

2-3
The Relationship of Theory, Research, and Application

The Role of Theory in Design

The Function of Theory

Theory helps us understand and interpret an observation before objective data has established it as a fact or intuitive experimentation has established it as useful. Theory is based on a belief usually rooted in observation, analysis, evaluation, and factual information, and sometimes in feelings, past experiences, or hunches. Theory both describes and predicts a usable method of working and outcome, and is particularly relevant in applied design activity where a form is disseminated to a broad audience.

Figure 2-3 illustrates the symbiotic relationship of theory, research, and application. Each aspect is related to and can influence the other. Hence, while the relationship is depicted as equilateral, with theory at the top, it can change depending on the problem to be solved and the inclination of the designer.

Many theories in the disciplines of design, the humanities, and science have influenced the creation and understanding of visual form. These theories generally fall into either modernist or postmodernist themes. The extent to which either category consciously influences designers is a point of debate and further illustrates the qualitative nature of design.

Modernism, as applied to visual form, has largely been furthered through teachings of the Bauhaus (an influential German design school, 1919–1933, that formalized a foundation of subjects and approach). Modernists seek universal truths that can be broadly applied, such as the meaning of shape or color. Postmodernism, a more recent movement, is founded in part on the writing of Jacques Derrida (1930–). He asserts that language and form are not neutral but carry cultural assumptions. Meaning is arbitrary, unstable, and has to be discovered by each reader. Forms based on this position seek to reveal many meanings of a single message and allow for multiple interpretations (see figure 6-3).

Theory of Human Perception

Perception and Gestalt Theory

Gestalt psychology began in Europe in the early 1900s, led by Swiss psychologist Max Wertheimer. This branch of psychology is important for understanding how we perceive visual form by organizing its components into a meaningful whole. Translated from German, *gestalt* means entire figure or configuration.

Gestalt's basic premise is that organization is central to all mental activity and is a reflection of how the brain functions. Using Gestalt, the whole is understood to be different from the sum of its parts.

A form that exhibits high organization has good gestalt, while a form with weak organization has weak gestalt. (*Good* in this sense means simple or regular and is not a value judgment.)

While becoming familiar with Gestalt may aid your ability to design more meaningfully, there is considerable debate among philosophers and psychologists about the validity or meaning of what we perceive. Is perception an objective act, or subjective? Is it innate or is it a product of our experiences and environment?

The principles of Gestalt are easily isolated, as shown in figures 2-5 through 2-8, but when combined and placed in context are influenced by factors such as the makeup of the audience and the environment in which the form is viewed. These factors can significantly affect the interaction and usefulness of each principle.

2-4
Cover for *The Dada Painters and Poets,* 1951
Paul Rand

This work relies on all four Gestalt principles to create a unified grouping and reflect the playful side of Dada (which means nonsense), an art movement from the early part of the twentieth century.

The Four Aspects of Gestalt

Gestalt's four aspects are closure, proximity, continuance, and similarity. Individually or collectively, these aspects help us understand form as a meaningful whole and not as isolated, unrelated parts.

CLOSURE

A form exhibits closure when its separate elements are placed so that you perceive the design as a whole rather than as disparate sections (figure 2-5).

CONTINUANCE

Continuance occurs when part of a form overlaps itself or an adjacent form. Your eye is led to follow the dominant form across the secondary without interruption (figure 2-6).

PROXIMITY

Proximity refers to distance between the parts comprising a form. In figure 2-7, the elements that are closer together appear to be related.

SIMILARITY

Similarity among parts in a form helps hold the form together and can be an effective way to create meaning. In figure 2-8, elements similar in size appear related.

2-5
Top, Left
Closure

2-6
Top, Right
Continuance

2-7
Bottom, Left
Proximity

2-8
Bottom, Right
Similarity

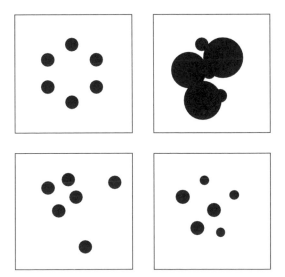

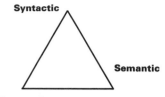

2-9

The Relationship Among the Three Parts of Semiotic Theory

Most meaningful and usable form combines each of the three aspects equally.

Theory of Creating and Evaluating Form

Semiotic Theory

Semiotic theory was first outlined in the 1930s by American philosopher Charles Morris, who believed that an analysis of visual and verbal signs could lead toward more effective communication. Semiotic theory is a branch of linguistics that has become a useful tool in two-dimensional design for understanding the relationship between the viewer/user, the form that conveys a message, and the message's meaning.

Figure 2-9 illustrates the symbiotic relationship of the three aspects of semiotic theory: syntactic, semantic, and pragmatic considerations. While each aspect can be examined separately, no one aspect is more important than the other; each works together and influences the other.

SYNTACTIC

Syntactic refers to the formal relationship among elements in a form or among related forms. When analyzing a form for its syntactic qualities, you might ask yourself: Are all parts of the form arranged to appear unified?

SEMANTIC

Semantic refers to the relationship between a form and its meaning. When analyzing a form for semantic qualities, you might ask yourself: Does the form adequately reflect its meaning? Is the meaning singular or multiple, ambiguous or clear? Which of these is more desirable?

PRAGMATIC

Pragmatic refers to the relationship between a form and its user. This aspect examines a sign when it is applied. When analyzing a form for its pragmatic qualities, consider these questions: Is the form related to its context? Is it understandable in its context?

2-10
Information Symbols from *Symbols Signs*, 1993
American Institute of Graphic Arts

Symbols from throughout the world that express common functions to varied audiences were collected and evaluated according to the three aspects of semiotic theory.

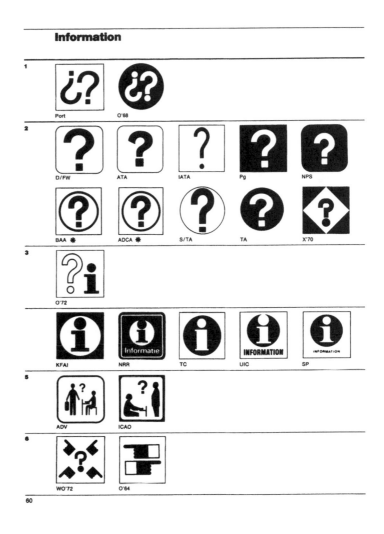

Information

2-11
Symbols and Corresponding Evaluation from *Symbols Signs*, 1993
American Institute of Graphic Arts

Each symbol was numerically evaluated and ranked accordingly.

Concept Description	Symbol Source	Evaluation			
		Semantic	Syntactic	Pragmatic	Group
1 **Pair of question marks.**	Port	3	3	3	3
	O'68	3	4	3	

Theory of Organizing and Understanding

Organizing Information

Alphabetical Listing
North America
South America

Alphabetical/Numerical Listing
1 North America
2 South America

2-12
Common Listing Methods

The way information is presented can suggest a value judgment.

Gaining and understanding information is vital to effective participation in the world. As the human population increases and technology accelerates, the amount of information grows exponentially, much of it transmitted via visual means. Information comes in the form of dates, times, locations, scientific relationships, and any expression that represents an attempt to come to terms with ourselves and others.

We receive information through a number of ways including the print and digital media, exchange with others, listening to our bodies (for example, feeling hot or cold as a signal of being sick), reference material, such as that commonly found in libraries or on the World Wide Web, and everyday observation and participation in the human-made and natural environment.

Our interpretation of information is influenced by the way it is organized (figure 2-12). Richard Saul Wurman, in *Information Anxiety*, notes five ways to organize information.[4]

ALPHABET

Alphabet refers to organization based on alphabetical order (figure 2-13).

CATEGORY

Category refers to organization based on types or models (figure 2-14).

CONTINUUM

Continuum refers to organization based on comparisons between or among elements (figure 2-14).

TIME

Time refers to organization based on the time or date of an event (figure 2-14).

LOCATION

Location refers to organization that identifies or orders where events, ideas, or other phenomena originate or occur (figure 2-15).

2-13
Pacific Bell White Pages, 1997
Matthew Carter (Font)
Pacific Bell Design (Page)

Alphabet

A problem may call for the use of a single method of organization. Alphabetic listings are useful for organizing large amounts of text-based information.

2-14
Morningstar Mutual Fund Report, 1997
Philip Burton

Category
Continuum
Time

Most work involves more than a single way of organizing information. This work uses multiple methods to organize both text and complex data.

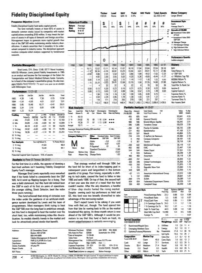

2-15
Map of the London Underground, 1933
Henry Beck

Location

Information can be presented through text alone or in combinations of text and graphic marks. This work, considered a hallmark in the field of information design, presents a highly complex network in a meaningful way.

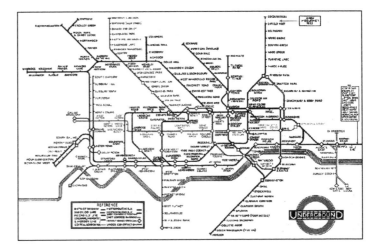

The Role of Methodology in Design

Purpose of Methodology

Methodology refers to the process of analyzing, defining, evaluating, or creating. Methodologies guide research by providing a structure for accomplishing something in a meaningful way; through them, investigations take form.

Methodologies can be structured, rational, and deliberate. These are in contrast to nonmethodical methods that are intuitive, loosely defined, and subconsciously applied. Most methodologies used in two-dimensional design are categorized as *problem-solving*. Problem-solving is generally linear, deductive (beginning with a broad view and narrowing down to a specific solution), and based on visual comparison among forms. It fosters critical thinking skills because it is a methodical procedure.

Methodologies used in some two-dimensional design activities are similar to those used in other disciplines. This is particularly evident when market tests or focus group observations (common in advertising) are performed on a design to be disseminated to a target audience.

A methodical procedure allows you to see where you've been, make comparisons among concepts, and better direct where you're going (figure 2-16). This can allow you to create more meaningful work and better articulate the work orally and in writing. While no method can ensure successful and insightful results, becoming aware of your working process and refining it can enhance your ability to work toward desired outcomes.

2-16
***Anticipation,* 1989**
Renee Crago Fisher

Initial Design (Top)
Refined Design (Middle)
Final Design (Bottom)

Hand-drawn patterns based on memories of a return to the ocean began a methodical process of exploration and refinement.

Types of Methodologies

Problem-Solving

Design activity is often referred to as a problem or series of problems. While the word *problem* in this context may seem negative, it actually signifies a challenge, an opportunity to create a successful and meaningful outcome.

The act of problem-solving involves identifying a problem or set of conditions, then arriving at an outcome in a consistent and enlightened manner. The problem is approached critically and deliberately rather than casually or passively. While a critical approach doesn't necessarily rule out chance or sudden inspiration, it does offer the opportunity to direct it.

Psychologists have studied problem-solving for much of this century. When broadly applied, it underlies all of life's activities. Problem-solving can be used to create a form or to create a method of organization or course of action. At its best, problem-solving is not reactive but proactive, anticipating future conditions or user traits. At its worst, problem-solving simply maintains conventions of form and ways of conveying information—even cultural stereotypes—without considering their implications.

2-17
Problem-Solving Exercise
Basic Design Students,
Stanford University

Problem-solving involves dialogue and compromise. Defining, sharing, and prioritizing individual and group needs is a way to become acquainted with the problem-solving process and develop empathy toward others. In this exercise, students were asked to list their needs, compare their commonality and importance, and note exchanges and steps taken during the process.

The Process of Problem-Solving

Psychologists have identified four steps that define the process of problem-solving. These steps can be approached in the order presented in figure 2-18. You can return at any time to one of the earlier steps; thus, problem-solving can be a circular or branching effort, as thinking is generally not linear.

LEARN CONDITIONS

Familiarize yourself with all aspects of the situation. Your focus should be directed to the work's audience and to the physical environment in which the work will exist.

IDENTIFY AND DEFINE THE PROBLEM

Examine the information gathered in the previous step. From this, you can determine the main issues and create a strategic plan that insightfully considers sources, all reasonable options, and their implications.

This step can involve visual diagramming: depicting ideas, concepts, needs, and relationships in pictorial form. Visual diagramming can better allow for the input of others in understanding and participating in the solution of a problem, and is useful when ideas are highly abstract or as yet undefined (figure 2-19).

GENERATE IDEAS AND SELECT SOLUTIONS

Search the possibilities and bring these to form (figure 2-20). Try to keep an open mind to all ideas, however seemingly inappropriate. Often an idea, or parts of an idea, becomes useful later as the project is further defined. From your ideas, choose one or several, depending on the application refine them, and decide on an outcome.

IMPLEMENT SOLUTION AND EVALUATE RESULT

The final step is to apply an outcome and evaluate the results of the process. Depending on the original problem, you can evaluate a solution through objective means, such as focus groups or market tests, that observe how people interact with a form. Or you can subjectively evaluate the solution through common sense and informal exchange with the audience. Ideally, the value of an outcome will have become evident earlier and this step confirms any expectations.

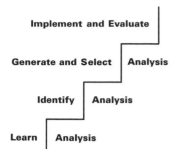

2-18
The Steps of Problem-Solving

Steps of problem-solving build upon one another, with analysis a part of the process at every step.

2-19
Visual Diagramming for Site Map of Web Site, 1997
Joy Panos Stauber, Collective

The following examples illustrate the process of designing a digital environment as a solution to presenting a wide range of information in an easily accessible and informative manner. Visual diagramming was used to evaluate sources of the problem and the roles of the audience, which in turn can help analyze existing relationships and design new ones.

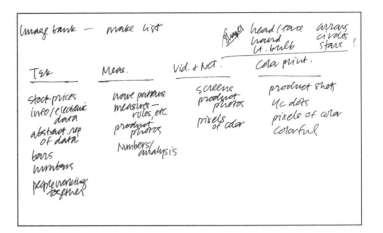

2-20
Early Iteration of Map of Web Site, 1997
Joy Panos Stauber, Collective

Clues to how things work are often revealed when their underlying structure is visually depicted.

2-21
Map and Informational Page of Web Site, 1997
Joy Panos Stauber and Eric Hillerns, Collective

The site map describes to the user the way to find products or specifications in the entire site. Information is organized according to type (continuum) and icons reflect Gestalt principles of similarity and closure.

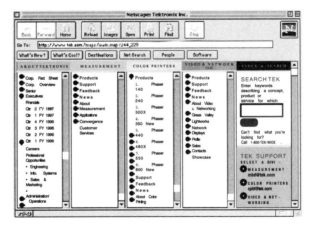

CHAPTER 3 | Elements and Interactions

Definitions and Analysis

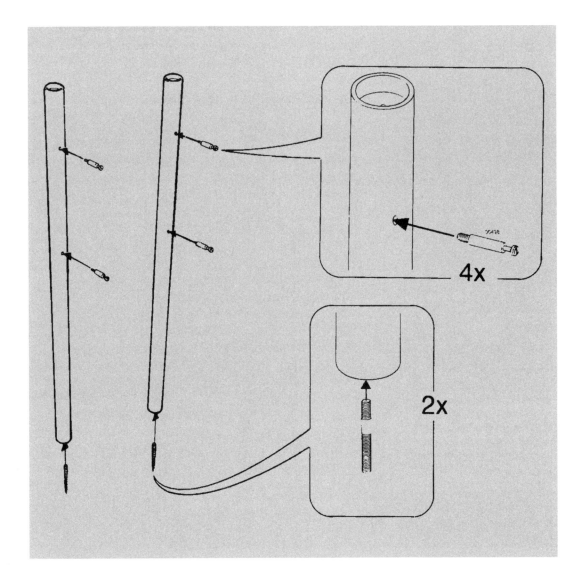

About This Chapter

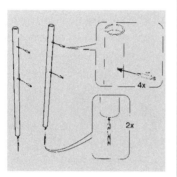

This chapter identifies and analyzes the basic visual components that create form and meaning.

Concepts and Terms in This Chapter

Presentations:

    Literal, Abstract, Symbolic

Form:

    Organic, Inorganic

Visual Elements:

    Dot, Line, Plane, Volume

Visual Characteristics:

    Size, Shape, Texture, Color

Visual Interactions:

    Position, Direction, Space

    (Negative Space,

    Depth, Perspective)

Balance:

    Visual Weight

    Symmetry, Asymmetry

3-1 (Previous page and above)
Instructional Diagram, 1995
IKEA

Basic elements such as lines can be used to group and separate information and direct action, as shown in this diagram for furniture assembly.

Defining Basic Visual Components

Visual Terms and Meanings

All visual form is made up of three categories of components: elements, characteristics, and interactions. Visual elements are dots, lines, planes, and volumes, and each element possesses characteristics of size, shape, texture, and color. These elements and characteristics are directed by principles of visual interaction, which are position, direction, and space.

These components can be identified and studied independently of one another, yet they are all simultaneously present in form and thus continually influence one another, even though a given form may emphasize one element, characteristic, or interaction.

We can evaluate the components by comparing them and by observing our position in relation to them. For example, we can determine the size of an object by comparing it to another object and in conjunction with our distance away.

When arranged and manipulated, elements, characteristics, and interactions result in a broad diversity of human-made and natural forms, both inorganic and organic. These forms represent ideas and concepts ranging from the literal to the symbolic.

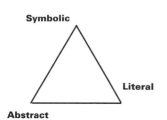

3-2
Three Ways of Presentation

Each way may be used separately or together in the creation of hybrid forms. The location of symbolic presentation at the top of the triangle does not suggest it is of greater value.

Ways of Describing Form

Presentations

Basic visual components can be used to create literal, abstract, or symbolic form (figures 3-3 through 3-5, respectively). These presentations take different approaches in conveying ideas and concepts, and serve different purposes.

The appropriateness of a presentation depends primarily on the subject to be depicted and the audience. Philosophical movements and cultural trends can influence the use of one over the other. For example, abstract form became a dominant means of presentation in the early twentieth century, based on discoveries and thinking that questioned accepted conventions across many disciplines. Abstraction furthered the ability to represent this thinking by departing from literal representation prevalent at the time.

LITERAL

Literal presentation presents an object or concept through detailed realism without unnecessary embellishment and exaggeration. It can be based on observation of an object and provide a record of subtleties in a complex form. This method allows the audience to understand the form through examination and comparison of its parts.

ABSTRACT

Abstract presentation involves deliberate simplification, often with exaggeration. This method can be based on observation of an object or can explore relationships among form alone, without direct observation. It is particularly useful for depicting difficult concepts, ideas, and observations because it excludes unimportant areas and focuses attention on parts critical to the meaning.

SYMBOLIC

Symbolic presentation uses symbols to convey complex technical information or highly abstract concepts that must be made clear to others. The symbols are generally not based on an object but are arbitrarily designed, with their meaning assigned and agreed upon, and learned by the audience. Symbolic representation is useful in mathematics, music, and many branches of science, and serves as the foundation of communication in these disciplines.

3-3

Illustrated Page Depicting Dispersion of Fruits and Seeds by the Wind, 1890
Designer Unknown

This literal drawing depicts what would otherwise be difficult to convey through symbolic or abstract means.

3-4

The Three Women, **1908**
Pablo Picasso

This abstract painting combines differing views of the same figures to further differing interpretations.

3-5

Operating Diagram of Electrical Substation, 1997
Michael Bowers

This symbolic drawing has coded meanings that must be learned in order for the drawing to be useful. Once learned, the representation conveys more meaning than would be possible in either a literal or abstract depiction.

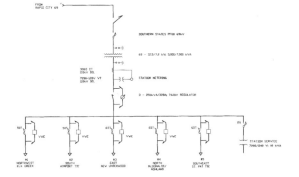

Types of Form

Geometric and Organic Form

Literal, abstract, and symbolic presentations can result in inorganic or organic form, or a combination of the two.

3-6
Basic Types of Geometric Form

Basic geometric forms such as the circle are often said to carry universally understood meanings such as unity, perfection and harmony. However, anecdotal evidence would suggest that such associations are generally only understood in individual situations.

GEOMETRIC

Inorganic form, more commonly called *geometric* form, has regular angles or patterns (figure 3-6). It is found in nature, as in the crystalline structures of rocks and snowflakes, and in human-made form when easy and memorable recognition is required (figure 3-7).

Geometric forms are made up of circles, triangles, squares, or combinations of these. Each shape has unique characteristics. Whereas the circle is equal in all directions, the lines of a square and a triangle continually move our eyes in various directions. For example, a square leads your eye up, down, and across. This might be useful when you need to guide eye movement in a particular direction.

ORGANIC

Organic form is fluid in appearance (figures 3-8, 3-9, and 3-10). Nature has an abundant supply of organic shapes and patterns that has long been an inspiration and source of objects of representation.

3-7
Stop Signs

We interpret messages in part based on their form, such as the octagon of a stop sign.

3-8, 3-9, 3-10
A Walk on the Beach,
Miami International Airport,
Concourse A, 1995
Michele Oka Doner

Saltwater plants and sea crea-
tures from South Florida
beaches were the inspiration
for this work. Two thousand
flat, bronze-cast elements were
embedded in the concourse
floor to reflect the movement
of the water toward and away
from the shore.

3-11
Dot

3-12
Line

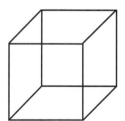

3-13
Plane

3-14
Volume

Defining Basic Visual Elements

Elements of Form

Whether geometric or organic, all form is built on basic elements: dots, lines, planes, and volumes.

DOT

A dot is the visual expression of a point, which is an indicator of location. A dot can take any shape, geometric or organic. It is generally simple in shape (figure 3-11).

LINE

A line is the connection of two or more dots that are so close they cannot be individually recognized (figure 3-12). It can be a continuous mark or a series of short dashed lines or separate dots visually connected by their similarity and placement. It can be straight or move in different directions. A line can also be a grouping of type, symbols, images, or simple markings.

Lines can create shapes and divide space. They are useful for isolating and grouping form and information. Depending on their appearance and position in a composition, along with the experiences we bring to viewing form, lines can connote emotional qualities.

PLANE

Plane refers to an area outlined by lines or defined by a grouping of images, type, symbols, or markings (figure 3-13). It is an expression of height or length and width.

The physical surface of a composition is often called the *picture plane.* Similar to dots and lines, a plane can be geometric or organic in shape.

VOLUME

Volume is a product of dots, lines and planes. It refers to the illusion of a three-dimensional form on a two-dimensional surface, and to the illusion of space within a form (space is discussed later in this chapter). Volume of the first type is created through the grouping of several dots, lines, or planes (figure 3-14).

3-15
***Self-Portrait,* 1977**
Chuck Close

Dots can be repeated and placed to create larger forms and meanings. Close uses dots as basic building components of identifiable forms that, while whole, maintain a sense of fragmentation.

3-16
***Heads,* 1995**
Kevin Donahue

Lines can describe the outline or contour of forms, their movements, and relationships. This work reveals the ability of lines in varying weight, length, and gesture to serve as the sole vehicle for describing mood and personality.

3-17
***Cartography,* 1996**
Sam Gilliam

Planes can be defined physically and by areas of markings or color that can appear to advance or recede, float or remain stationary.

3-18
Size

3-19
Shape

3-20
Texture

Defining Basic Visual Characteristics

Characteristics of Form

Whether literal, abstract, or symbolic, organic or geometric, all two-dimensional form has visual characteristics. Visual characteristics are size, shape, texture, and color.

SIZE

We understand the size of a form in relation to other objects or the environment in which the form is placed (figure 3-18).

We can also determine the size of a form by measuring its length or height. The term *scale* is often used in the process of making size comparisons. We make such comparisons in reference to familiar forms or to our own height or width.

SHAPE

Shape refers to the external outline of a form (figure 3-19).

TEXTURE

In two-dimensional form, texture is visual and not tactile. Visual texture can be defined as the sum of visual components that create a plane recognizable as a unified grouping. All two-dimensional forms portray a texture however subtle or pronounced (figure 3-20).

COLOR

Color (as relating to hue) has many unique characteristics, and is discussed in the next chapter. One characteristic of color that is present in the corresponding figures is value (light and dark). Figures 3-18, 3-19, and 3-20 exhibit a value range of black, white and grey.

3-21
Poster for Steamship Line, 1931
Adolphe Mouron Cassandre

Dramatic size differences between elements (and the angle in which elements are depicted) can create a sense of power and awe.

3-22
Signage and Billboards

The physical size of a form can influence our understanding of a message.

3-23
Nike Symbol, 1972
Carolyn Davidson

Shape alone can serve as the identifier of a message through repeated exposure and learned association.

3-24
***Mural,* 1943**
Jackson Pollock

Repeated markings create texture and movement and in Pollock's work, serve as a record of the physical energy of creation.

**3-25
Frame**

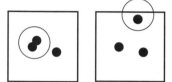

**3-26
Position and
Tension Points (Circled)**

**3-27
Cropping**

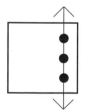

**3-28
Direction and
Eye Movement (Arrow)**

Defining Basic Visual Interactions

Interactions of Form

Visual elements interact through position, direction, and space. Taken together or separately, these principles of interaction govern the placement of elements and influence our understanding of meaning.

Visual elements and their characteristics are arranged in relation to the area or frame in which they appear (figure 3-25). A frame marks the limits of a form. It can take any shape and greatly influences a composition. For example, a square frame, equal on all sides, does not dictate an emphasis to a grouping of elements it contains.

POSITION

Position refers to the placement of an element relative to other elements and/or the frame. Overlapping, touching, or not touching are basic ways that elements can be positioned.

The distance between elements and between elements and the frame can create points of focus and tension. By positioning an element close to the frame edge or another element, you can heighten a relationship between the two (figure 3-26).

The perception and meaning of an element can be altered depending on its relationship to the frame. It can appear in its entirety (figure 3-26) or be cropped (figure 3-27). Cropping can create a sense of movement and suggest that the compositional area extends beyond the frame.

DIRECTION

Direction refers to a course of movement. Horizontal, vertical, and diagonal lines of any angle move our eye in a given direction (figure 3-28). While elements placed in parallel directions further similarity, contrasting can create focal points and movement in a composition.

3-29
***Identity Image,* 1997**
Johnson and Wolverton

Overlapping planes create a
sense of movement and suggest a thematic relationship
among the objects and typography of the vernacular landscape. The low resolution
heightens the objects grittiness
and furthers a merging of similar lines and color.

3-30
**Poster for the Rural
Electrification
Administration, 1937**
Lester Beall

Direction can reinforce elements in a form and heighten
an intended meaning. The
background stripes imply a flag
and echo the lines of the fence
to create a direct and cohesive
statement of stability, strength,
and national pride.

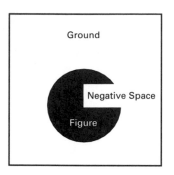

3-31
Figure/Ground Relationship

Space is perhaps the most important aspect of interaction in a composition. The areas between and around elements are active participants in the composition, and can be as dominant and important as the elements themselves. Space can group, separate, and emphasize elements and allow the viewer to better distinguish elements and their roles in a composition.

The terms *figure* and *ground* are used to describe a perception of spatial interaction. Figure refers to an element on the picture plane, while ground is the larger area surrounding it (figure 3-31).

Psychologists have studied the figure-ground relationship and have found that we understand form if it is distinguishable from the background. This is generally done through a difference in value between the figure and the ground. The term *negative space* refers to a seemingly empty but active area of a composition. By virtue of being surrounded by elements in the composition, a negative area can appear to come forward and be slightly brighter than the surrounding background, as in figure 3-31.

3-32
Publication Cover, 1996
Matt Eller, Walker Art Center

Space around elements can help to define and emphasize objects and give meaning to the entire form. The positioning of the letters (from a font designed by the central figure) seek to echo their visual qualities and variations.

3-33
Venus, 1952
Henri Matisse

Space can become active
through its shape and position
in the composition, and evoke
association and movement.

3-34
**Page from *The Composing
Room*, 1960**
Chermayeff and Geismar

The simple integration of
shapes through negative and
positive areas can create a
cohesive and engaging form.

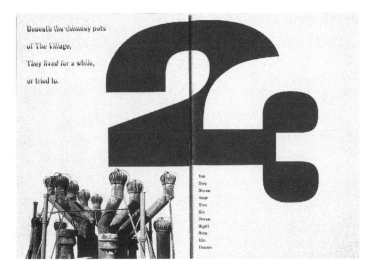

Elements of Compositional Interaction

Depth and Perspective

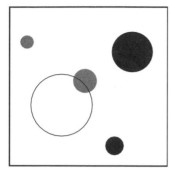

3-35
Depth by Overlapping, Size, and Value

Most depictions of depth use more than a single pictorial cue.

Depth in a composition can create contrast and help a form communicate its purpose and meaning. In three-dimensional design, depth is physically present; in two-dimensional design, however, an *illusion* of depth must be created through pictorial cues (visual representations that signal differences or direct understanding), including color and value changes, size, overlapping, and perspective (figure 3-35).

Perspective is created through the use of lines to depict three-dimensional form on a flat, two-dimensional surface. In linear perspective, which is the most common method, objects are foreshortened (tapered) to give the illusion that they recede in space toward a common point (figure 3-37).

Perspective is a distinctly Western invention, refined during the Renaissance as an aid in organizing compositional space and in lending order to our relationship to the environment. Eastern cultures have not traditionally relied on perspective to depict depth; when lines are present, they are often parallel. This tends to create an impression rather than an optical description (figure 3-38).

3-36
Field of Sunflowers

Depth is created through pictorial cues of diminishing size, overlapping of forms, and increasing haze in the distance.

3-37
Ideal City, Named the City of God, fifteenth century
Piero della Francesca

Lines converging on a single point create a strong sense of depth and order, positioning the viewer in front of the scene.

3-38
The Road to Shu, 1858
Hine Taizan

Vast open space, depth, and strong sense of scale reflects a reverence for the land.

3-39
Mutual Fund Report, 1994
Lisa Strausfeld
Massachusetts Institute of Technology Media Lab

Perspective can create a sense of movement among forms and can be used to prioritize ideas and information.

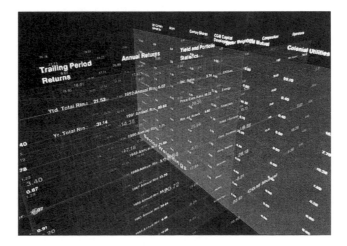

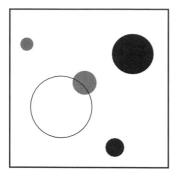

3-40

Equilibrium through Asymmetrical Balance

The heavy black dots are balanced by the larger outlined dot and position of the lighter grey dots.

Visual Weight and Balance

Visual weight is the sum of a form's components and is akin to mass and energy. However, visual weight is not easily identified because it cannot be touched or physically measured. In addition, our perception of visual weight is influenced by a range of variables including size and color (figure 3-40).

Visual balance refers to the degree of equilibrium in a composition. This is determined by the choice and arrangement of elements in relation to each other and the frame. Position is the dominant means of creating balance, resulting in symmetry, asymmetry, or combinations of both.

SYMMETRY

A form has symmetry when it can be divided diagonally, vertically, or horizontally and the resulting sides are essentially the same. While there are numerous types of symmetry, each varies in the number and location of divisions. Bilateral symmetry (two equal halves) is the most common type of symmetry (figure 3-41). Symmetric balance tends to create a stable form, keeping your eye in a general location.

Symmetry is abundant in nature and is the oldest method of seeking visual balance. The ancient Egyptians, Greeks, Mayans and Romans sought balance through symmetry in order to find and reveal order not only in the visual realm but also in religion and philosophy.

ASYMMETRY

A form has asymmetry when it is divided and the resulting sides are not the same size and shape (figure 3-43). This is also called *dynamic tension* or *dynamic equilibrium,* and refers to organization based on juxtaposition (the placement of visually or conceptually contrasting forms in close proximity to each other). Asymmetric balance can create a active form, forcing your eye around and through a composition.

Many Eastern cultures have used asymmetry for centuries, particularly in architecture and interior design. For much of the twentieth century asymmetry has been used in the West, and most recently, combinations of asymmetry and symmetry have been used extensively by many disciplines in both the East and the West as a new way of representing new ideas, including those political and social in nature.

3-41
Pages from a Book of Hours, 1543
Simon de Colines

Symmetry in form can support symmetry in life. Books of this type were used to direct prayer at given hours throughout the day. Supporting ritual is a common design function.

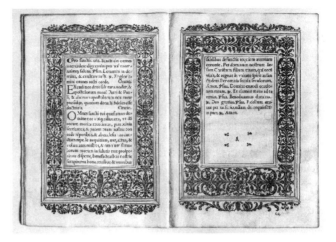

3-42
Stanzas from "The Crab Canon" from *The Musical Offering*, 1747
JS Bach

When graphically depicted, nonvisual expressions often readily reveal asymmetry and symmetry as evident in this piece that exhibits aspects of the latter.

3-43
***Composition with Red, Yellow, and Blue,* 1930**
Piet Mondrian

Asymmetry can create a sense of movement among elements in a form. This work is an example from the Dutch de Stijl movement (at its peak during World War I) a leading force in the experimentation with and advocacy of asymmetry.

CHAPTER 4

Color
Types, Interactions, and Roles

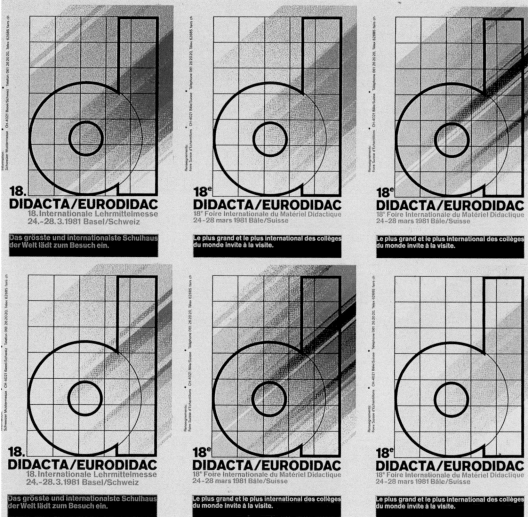

About This Chapter

This chapter discusses the types and basic properties of color and its ability to create meaning and identity.

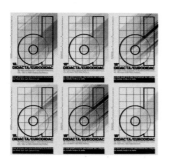

Concepts and Terms in This Chapter

Color

Additive/Subtractive Color

Primaries/Secondaries

Complementary Colors

Analogous/Discordant Colors

Hue

Value/Intensity

Temperature

Relativity

Proportions

Identity

4-1 (Previous page and above)
Color Studies, 1981
Wolfgang Weingart

Color alone can alter the appearance and meaning of a form. One letter from these studies was used in figure 4-2.

The Use of Color

Color as an Active Component

Similar to other visual components, color can help create meaning. But because color is a property of light, it has many additional and unique characteristics and interactions.

In the late 1600s, Sir Isaac Newton experimented with simple glass prisms and found that sunlight is made up of color. Without light there is no color, because objects have no color of their own. However, objects possess properties that absorb or reflect particular light waves, which become visible to our eyes. For example, we perceive the color red when light waves of a certain frequency strike or bounce off of a surface and are transmitted to our eyes.

Our understanding of a form's color is influenced by a number of variables, including the type and intensity of lighting on the object viewed, our distance away, learned color associations, and surrounding colors. Thus, the definition of color is relative to and dependent on cultural and physical context.

Color can be used to depict things as they are, as in the local color of green for grass. It can also be used without reference to observed objects to connect us to more abstract or symbolic ideas or meanings. Color can create the perception of volume and depth. It can be used to group elements and concepts, emphasize them, and enhance our understanding in ways that black and white may not. Similar to other components, color can stimulate a range of memories and expectations.

4-2
Poster for a Conference on Education, 1981
Wolfgang Weingart

4-3
**Additive Primaries:
Red-Orange, Green,
Blue-Violet**

4-4
**Subtractive Primaries:
Red, Yellow, Blue**

4-5
**Subtractive Primaries in
Offset Printing: Cyan,
Magenta, Process Yellow,
and Black**

Defining Color

Types of Color

In each of the two types of color (described below) are basic colors called *primaries* from which all other colors are made. These primaries vary with the color's source.

ADDITIVE COLOR

Additive color is viewed directly as light, such as that emitted by a computer monitor. Its primaries are red-orange, green, and blue-violet (figure 4-3). When these primaries are positioned or added in equal amounts, white light—the source of all color—is created.

Computer monitors create the illusion of a range of colors by activating dots (pixels) to red, green, or blue in varying levels of intensity (brightness/dullness). These are mixed optically by our eyes to create additional colors and forms. White is produced when pixels are at maximum intensity and appear to overlap.

SUBTRACTIVE COLOR

Subtractive color is viewed as a reflection off a surface. In subtractive color, all light waves except those containing the color we see are absorbed or subtracted by a surface. We see the color red when its corresponding wavelength is reflected to our eyes.

One type of subtractive color is created through pigments. Pigments have primary colors of red, yellow, and blue (figure 4-4).

Another type of subtractive color occurs in offset printing, the most common printing method. The colors cyan, magenta, and yellow, in conjunction with black (CMYK), are used in varying dot sizes and numbers to create the appearance of other colors (figure 4-5, figure 4-6). Separate colored dots are not physically mixed but instead mixed by our eyes to create larger areas of color. In this book, violet is a combination of magenta and cyan dots.

4-6
Detail of Figure 4-1

When an offset printed image is magnified the use of CMYK dots becomes more readily apparent.

4-7
A Sunday Afternoon on the Island of La Grande Jatte, 1884–1886
Georges Seurat

Using a method similar to offset printing, small dots of color were applied to create larger color areas. This technique creates an impression rather than a literal depiction by allowing the eye to optically mix the separate dots of colors.

Presentations of Color Relationships

Organization

The relationship of primary colors to secondary colors is easily depicted through the form commonly called a *color wheel* (figures 4-8 and 4-9). Secondary colors are mixtures of two primaries. Some color wheels include tertiary and additional subgroupings. Because not all colors have the same strength (some primaries are inherently darker or lighter, brighter or duller, than others), mixtures to make secondaries may not be equal.

Numerous varieties of color wheels have been made throughout history. Other influential systems of color organization, including those by Johann Wolfgang Goethe, depict colors in different shapes or identify them by different names. What remains constant is the positioning of colors. For example, red is always between orange and violet, a relationship resulting from their natural properties.

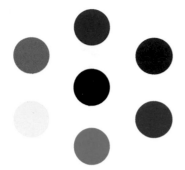

4-8
Subtractive Color Wheel

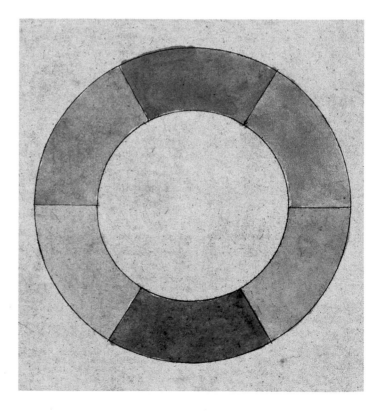

4-9

Color Study from *Zür Farbenlehre*, 1810
Johann Wolfgang Goethe

Early depiction of color relationships.

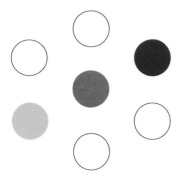

4-10
Complementary Colors

Color Strategies

Color Palettes

Color can be used a part of a strategy to organize form, send messages, and create response. Compositions are commonly designed using specific color palettes or families to create harmony or discord appropriate to the message.

COMPLEMENTARY COLORS

Complementary colors are opposite from each other on the color wheel. In figure 4-10, violet and yellow are complements. When mixed, they create a neutral gray; when placed next to each other, their intensity is heightened (see figure 4-21).

ANALOGOUS AND DISCORDANT COLORS

Analogous colors are adjacent to each other on the color wheel (figure 4-11), while discordant colors are farther apart but not directly across from one another. Generally speaking, analogous colors tend to create harmony among elements (figure 4-12) and discordant colors create instability and movement. Either type of color combination is desirable depending on the situation.

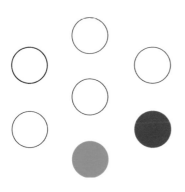

4-11
Analogous Colors

4-12
***Water Lilies,* 1914–1915**
Claude Monet

This work, based on analogous colors of green and blue, creates harmony among the elements.

4-13
Hue

4-14
Value

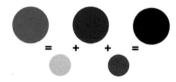

4-15
Value and Intensity

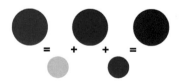

4-16
**Value, Intensity, and
Temperature**

The Basic Components of Color

Hue, Value, Intensity, and Temperature

Subtractive and additive color have four basic qualities: hue, value, intensity, and temperature.

HUE

Hue refers to a pure color with no other colors, black, or white added to it. In figures 4-13, 4-15 and 4-16, the same hue appears in the center dot. Its appearance changes according to alterations in value, intensity, and temperature. The size of the smaller dots in the latter two figures only generalizes the amount of color needed to make the color of the larger dots.

VALUE

Value refers to the lightness or darkness of a color. You shade a hue by adding black and tint a hue by adding white. The term *achromatic* applies to mixtures of black and white only (figure 4-14), while *monochromatic* applies to mixtures based on shades and tints of a single hue (figure 4-15). The center gray dot (figure 4-14) has approximately the same amount of white as the center red dot directly below it (figure 4-15). In figures 4-15 and 4-16, the left dots are lighter in value and the right dots are darker in value.

INTENSITY

Intensity or *saturation* refers to the brightness or dullness of a color. A color is at full intensity or purity only when it is unmixed. Intensity and value are related because a color's intensity changes when black, white, or another color is added. In figures 4-15 and 4-16, the center red dot is more intense (brighter) than the dots on either side. When the center dot is mixed with a light gray or a light color such as yellow, it becomes less intense (duller) and lighter. When mixed with a dark gray or dark color such as blue, it becomes duller and darker.

TEMPERATURE

Temperature refers to the relative warmth or coolness of a color. We generally think of red, orange, and yellow as warm, and blue, green, and violet as cool. But any color, even red, can be warm or cool depending on the type and amount of other colors added. In figure 4-16, yellow is added to the center red dot to make it warm, and blue is added to make it cool.

4-17
Late Reminder (from
Homage to the Square),
1953
Josef Albers

Changes in hue, value, intensity, and temperature in simple proportions can create a sense of depth and focus and alone serve as subject matter.

4-18
**Poster for the Basle
Theater, 1968**
Armin Hofmann

A cool red (left side) and warm
red (right) were used to suggest the contrast of work to be
shown at the theater.

Color Interactions

Relativity

Perceptually, color is highly relative. Similar to other visual elements, such as size, we understand color in relation to its environment.

A color can be perceived differently depending on its surrounding colors. In figure 4-19, the mixture of the gray dot is constant, yet it appears lighter against the black background, darker and duller on the white background, and lighter and brighter on the violet background.

The violet background also makes the dot appear to contain yellow, the complement of violet. This phenomenon, known as *simultaneous contrast,* is a result of the physiological mechanics of our eyes. Being aware of this phenomenon may be useful when using certain color combinations to achieve desired ends.

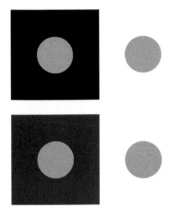

4-19
Perceptual Relativity

The perception of hue, value, intensity, temperature, and even size are influenced by the surrounding color.

4-20
East Window of Dorchester Abbey, twelfth century
Dorchester-on-Thames, Oxfordshire, England

The black leading between the pieces of glass heightens the brightness of the colors and in turn the message and experience they support.

4-21
Proportions

By changing the proportions of these complementary colors, the overall relationship is affected.

Proportions

Proportions in color are defined, in part, through size. They can also be created through the use of value, intensity, and temperature. Using these, numerous attempts have been made to assign size proportions to colors. For example, three units of yellow to one unit of violet, two units of orange to one unit of blue, and one unit of green to one unit of red have been deemed visually balanced and harmonious.[1] However, the appropriateness of these ratios relies on the context and the surroundings, and thus is open to debate.

The proportions of a color can greatly change the appearance of a color grouping (figure 4-21). Depending on the colors, a seemingly harmonious composition can move to a state of discord, and vice versa.

Proportions are an important consideration when seeking to create diversity through a limited palette. In figure 4-23, a basic palette was chosen and its colors used in varying proportions across a number of applications. This gives each application a unique identity while retaining a connection to the palette.

4-22
Poster for Library Campaign, 1992
Lucille Tenazas

The thoughtful arrangement of a limited range of colors allows this composition to further its appearance and message.

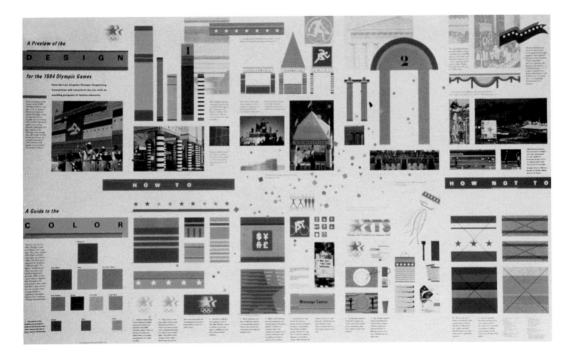

4-23
Color Palette for the Los Angeles Olympiad, 1984
Sussman/Prejza and Company

Color as Meaning

Forming Response and Identity

Although humans perceive color interactions similarly, we each have different interpretations of their meanings. Akin to other visual elements discussed earlier, most attributes of color are understood in relation to the environment in which they exist and are interpreted through the experiences of the designer and viewer (figure 4-24).

A color's perceptual interactions, discussed earlier, are easily seen and thus more objectively discussed than its connotations. To use color meaningfully and effectively, it is important to be aware that color carries connotations. This may lead you to research a work's audience, the current and historical uses of the colors, and the context in which the color will be used.

Some colors carry similar meanings across cultures. Red, for example, connotes danger in most cultures. Other colors are interpreted differently. Death and mourning, for example, are associated with the color black in the West but the color white in China.

We also associate color with our natural environment. We perceive red, orange, and yellow as warm perhaps because of their relationship to fire and sunlight. Violet, green, and blue are perceived as cool perhaps because of their relationship to sky and water. Such associations, as well as color preferences, have been shown in controlled studies to be influenced not only by culture but also age and gender, and the form or shape through which a color is experienced.[3]

Color can be used to convey information and relationships. In business, black indicates gain and red indicates loss. Color can place value on activities, such as a blue ribbon awarded for excellence. Color can also create a sense of identity and community, as evidenced by the common practice among organizations, corporations, and other entities to select, display, and market their own colors. In figure 4-25, the flag's colors symbolize the diversity of the gay and lesbian community with red, orange, yellow, green, indigo, and violet representing life, healing, sun, serenity with nature, harmony, and spirit respectively.[4]

4-24
Nulli Secundus, 1963
Hans Hofmann

The interplay among contrasting hues, values, intensities,
and temperatures can create
connotations and emotional
responses.

4-25
The Rainbow Gay Flag, 1978
Gilbert Baker

Color can build a sense of
community and identity.

CHAPTER 5 | Composition
Shaping Appearance and Understanding

About This Chapter

This chapter examines how visual components can be organized to create desired appearances and meanings.

Concepts and Terms in This Chapter

Composition

Harmony

Simplicity/Complexity

Order/Chaos

Attention/Hierarchy

Contrast

Rhythm/Sequencing

Repetition

Pattern

Proportions

Structure

Geometry/Ratios

5-1 (Previous page and above)
Amish Split-Bars Quilt, Lancaster County, Pennsylvania, 1900
Designer Unknown

Even the simplest forms can exhibit thoughtful use of basic visual elements, characteristics, and interactions.

Defining Composition

Composing Visually

Composition refers to the arrangement of elements and characteristics within a defined area. This arrangement can be both visually pleasing but, more importantly, used to convey specific information and meaning.

Visual composition is similar to composition in other activities such as writing and music. In these activities we seek harmony. The word *harmony* has Greek origins (harmos: to join) and, in a visual context, it indicates a grouping of related components that make sense together. While harmony can involve some degree of discord or tension that attracts us, it is balanced by an overall appearance of continuity, of organized visual movement. A form that balances change with a level of consistency among its parts is often visually engaging and meaningful.

A form's composition can emphasize parts of information, reveal relationships among components, and guide interpretation. This can be done by making some aspects more dominant than others to create different levels of attention. Structure can also be used to create order and unity, and to guide meaning. These considerations can be addressed in a single composition or across several compositions that are seen together as a group.

Philosophies of Visual Organization

Simplicity and Complexity

The term *simplicity* usually refers to a form with a limited number of simple, elements (figure 5-2), or a form that is organized in such a way that its message is unambiguous and easily understood.

Certain ideas or objects depicted in abstract, symbolic, or literal form require some degree of simplification. This is particularly evident in the design of symbols, such as those shown in chapter 2, where information is often more effectively understood if visually simplified. In such a context, simplification heightens relationships among parts of a form by reducing the number of parts used. Yet, when a form is visually simplified it can actually become conceptually complex and enriched. Hence, simplicity should not be construed as simplistic.

Simplicity has also served as an identifier of cultures such as the Shakers. Founded in Massachusetts in the 19th century, simplicity in their lifestyle and design was an expression of communal religious beliefs. And while simplicity has been a dominant theme in design for much of the twentieth century, recently its widespread use has been questioned. Technology allows increased manipulation of imagery and typography, and attitudes toward the role and meaning of ornamentation have changed as part of the cyclical nature of thinking.

The adage "less is more" has its place under certain conditions, but should not be taken as a mandate to eliminate ornamentation. Introducing complexity is not necessarily a deliberate effort to make something confusing. Complexity can reveal the richness and subtleties of an idea. The work in figure 5-3 appears visually complex even though its message seems clear. As with simplicity, complexity's desirability in a form is dependent on the context.

"Less is More"[1]
(circa 1947)

Mies Van der Rohe

"Less is a Bore"[2]
(circa 1966)

Robert Venturi

"More is different"[3]
(circa 1997)

Dr. Philip W. Anderson

5-2
***The A–Z Book,* 1969**
Thomas Ockerse

This book contains a series of die-cut shapes examining relationships among letters of the Roman alphabet. The adjacent pages reveal the letter *V* found in the letter *M.*

Pages 1, 2   **Pages 3, 4**

Order and Chaos

Order has long been a human concern, from the days of early Egypt to the present. Design, by most definitions, is an activity that involves or seeks some degree of order. For the most part, our needs are met through meaningful organization and not those chaotic in nature. Organization is a common tendency in our lives. We generally exhibit patterns of order over randomness in our daily activities. Order can bring clarity and result in a better understanding of purpose.

What defines chaos is open to interpretation as well as when it is appropriate. Many apparently chaotic and complex systems possess orderly structures and intent. Figure 5-3 is an active, chaotic composition, yet further examination reveals order based on aligned horizontal lines and merged areas of similar value. The balance between chaos and order suggests a progression of ideas and change, and reinforces the subject matter.

5-3
U.S. Postal Stamp Commemorating the 19th Amendment, 1995
April Greiman

Seemingly chaotic and active forms are often structured through the alignment of common elements and characteristics such as colors, basic shapes, and type.

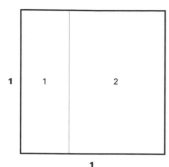

5-4
External and Internal Proportions

Determining a format and dividing it with reference to the material to be presented, is an early step in the creation of a message.

Ways of Finding Relationships

Proportions

Proportions help describe the visual forms we see each day, from buildings to household objects. They also represent the nonvisual, such as the amount of time we work in a given day. Whether in visual or nonvisual form, proportions can be compared, measured, and analyzed.

In visual form, the term *proportion* refers to the size relationship between parts of a form. Width and height can be compared to determine proportions in a two-dimensional form. Such a comparison might examine the relationship between the form's external dimensions as well as its internal dimensions (figure 5-4). For example, the width and height of this page are external dimensions, while the width of this text column and the white space to the left are internal dimensions.

In addition to creating harmony, proportions can help us make sense of our place in the universe. To some, harmonious form suggests the expression of a higher order or that the universe is in order. Although proportions can make a form more visually inviting, they can also enhance functionality (figure 5-5) and the communication of meaning, and can be used to persuade or create a desired impression (figure 5-6).

5-5
Diagrams from *The Measure of Man,* 1955
Henry Dreyfuss Associates

These diagrams reveal the basic proportions of some human bodies. These, and others, have been used for the design of a variety of industrial products from chairs to automobiles.

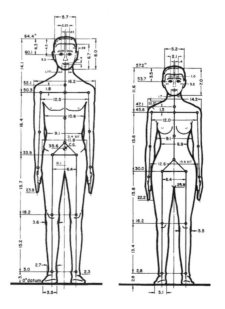

5-6
Palette of Narmer, 3000 B.C.

The Palette of Narmer depicts a king who once controlled the region of present-day Egypt. Note the king's exaggerated proportions and size relative to his subjects.

Finding and Using Proportions

The first reference point in finding and understanding proportions is the human body. Your height (and what it allows you to see) and the length of your arms (and how far you can reach) are two continual factors that influence how you understand and interact with the things around you.

For centuries, the human body has served as the model for measuring and understanding the world. The fathom, which is the length of an average man's outstretched arms, was developed by the Greeks in 600 B.C. as a way of measuring distances. The metric system, based on units of ten (ten centimeters in a meter, ten meters in a kilometer, and so on), relates to our ten fingers.

Perhaps the best-known study of human body proportions was done during the Renaissance by Leonardo da Vinci (Italian, 1452–1519), who examined and compared parts of the body in relation to basic geometric shapes. His studies sought to find a system of proportions usable for architecture and for the depiction of human form (figure 5-7).

5-7
Proportional Study, mid-fifteenth century
Leonardo da Vinci

The figure's proportions are based on those described by Vitruvius as normal for an adult male.

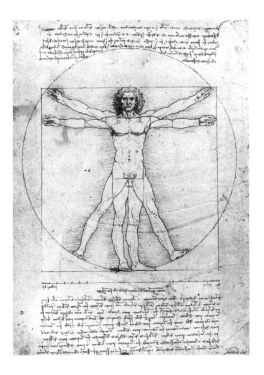

Ways of Directing Understanding

Attention and Hierarchy

Capturing, maintaining, and focusing attention are important considerations in strengthening the appearance and meaning of a form. The choice and arrangement of components can lead our eye in a particular direction and keep it there or encourage it to move on.

Attention can be drawn through the use of hierarchy, in which some components or ideas stand out before others when arranged in dominant and subordinate areas. A dominant area is called the *focal point* (figure 5-8).

Hierarchy can make a composition more active and engaging, and aid the viewer in discerning which elements belong together. When some elements are presented over others, it is easier to understand the whole form and its function.

Research into how the human eye examines complex objects suggests that we are attracted primarily to elements in a composition we consider important and essential to understanding[5] (figure 5-9). While such research can aid your ability to compose, it is important to note that scientific studies are generally conducted in controlled environments and that their outcomes are difficult to apply broadly. Many variables influence attention, including the physical environment in which a work is viewed or used, and one's cultural background, which may condition responses to shape and color.

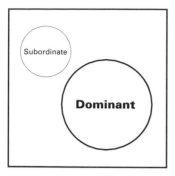

5-8
Hierarchy through Size and Position

Although an element placed at the top of a composition can suggest greater importance relative to other elements, it may not be the first element viewed. Dominance and importance depends on a number of other variables, including size.

5-9
Page from *Eye Movements and Reading Orders*, 1967
Dr. Alfred L. Yarbus

This time-lapse record of eye movement shows how we concentrate on the most informative and characteristic aspects of form.

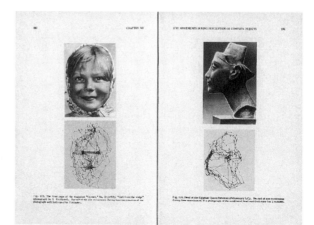

5-10
***Emiliano Zapata,* 1995**
Mauricio Lasansky

A focal point (the eyes in this
example) can contribute to the
character of a work.

5-11
**Order Form for *Emigre,*
1997**
Rudy Vanderlans

Viewing order and usage can
be directed by the use of simple visual elements and grouping. In this form, repeated dots,
and lines common in size and
alignment, define clearly identifiable sections, each with its
own function.

Contrast

Attention and hierarchy are created through contrast, which refers to differences among elements and their degree of conflict or discord. We experience, desire, and create contrast daily for purposes of enrichment and identity as expressed in the clothes we wear. Contrast can also serve as an important tool of recognition as evidence by road signs whose color is generally in stark contrast their surroundings. In the animal world, contrasts of movement, color, and pattern are an aid to survival as they often signal danger and initiate action.

Contrast can be achieved through opposing visual elements such as shape, direction, and color (figure 5-12). The interactions among contrasting elements are analogous to those in the physical realm. Although physical forces such as gravity are perceivable and thus more evident, visual forces are only observable.

We tend to favor compositions in which the parts are related in some way but also have differences, however subtle or pronounced. Contrast can attract and maintain our attention and move our eye to specific areas. It can reveal relationships and help us differentiate information. Organizing information according to contrast can also be a way of making qualitative judgments, as discussed in chapter 2.

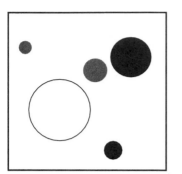

5-12
Contrast
Big/Small
Light/Dark
Close/Distant

5-13
***Hanging Out at Carmine Street*, 1996**
David Carson

Contrast can create active movement and reflect the subject matter. The placement of the dominant text defies the convention of a linear reading order used in Western cultures (top to bottom, left to right) to further its meaning.

5-14
***Exercise in Contrast,* 1967**
Emil Ruder

Changes in shape and value
can create contrast, texture,
and movement. Univers is a
typeface whose simplicity and
uniformity among weights
allows for unified groupings
and clear transmission of ideas.

UniversUniversUniversUniversUniversUniversUniversUnivers
UniversUniversUniversUniversUniversUniversUniversUnivers
UniversUniversUniversUniversUniversUniversUniversUnivers
UniversUniversUniversUniversUniversUniversUniversUnivers
UniversUniversUniversUniversUniversUniversUniversUnivers
UniversUniversUniversUniversUniversUniversUniversUnivers
UniversUniversUniversUniversUniversUniversUniversUnivers
UniversUniversUniversUniversUniversUniversUniversUnivers
UniversUniversUniversUniversUniversUniversUniversUnivers
UniversUniversUniversUniversUniversUniversUniversUnivers
UniversUniversUniversUniversUniversUniversUniversUnivers
UniversUniversUniversUniversUniversUniversUniversUnivers
UniversUniversUniversUniversUniversUniversUniversUnivers
UniversUniversUniversUniversUniversUniversUniversUnivers
UniversUniversUniversUniversUniversUniversUniversUnivers
UniversUniversUniversUniversUniversUniversUniversUnivers
UniversUniversUniversUniversUniversUniversUniversUnivers
UniversUniversUniversUniversUniversUniversUniversUnivers
UniversUniversUniversUniversUniversUniversUniversUnivers
UniversUniversUniversUniversUniversUniversUniversUnivers
UniversUniversUniversUniversUniversUniversUniversUnivers
UniversUniversUniversUniversUniversUniversUniversUnivers
UniversUniversUniversUniversUniversUniversUniversUnivers
UniversUniversUniversUniversUniversUniversUniversUnivers
UniversUniversUniversUniversUniversUniversUniversUnivers
UniversUniversUniversUniversUniversUniversUniversUnivers
UniversUniversUniversUniversUniversUniversUniversUnivers
UniversUniversUniversUniversUniversUniversUniversUnivers
UniversUniversUniversUniversUniversUniversUniversUnivers
UniversUniversUniversUniversUniversUniversUniversUnivers
UniversUniversUniversUniversUniversUniversUniversUnivers
UniversUniversUniversUniversUniversUniversUniversUnivers
UniversUniversUniversUniversUniversUniversUniversUnivers
UniversUniversUniversUniversUniversUniversUniversUnivers

5-15
***The Church at Picuris
Pueblo, New Mexico,* 1963**
Laura Gilpin

Contrast can create a focal
point and heighten the meaning of a composition.

Creating and Organizing Multiple Forms

Rhythm

The natural environment provides an abundance of physical forms, patterns, and movements that establish rhythms. Since the beginning of recorded history, nature has influenced the creation of human-made rhythms. For example, the Nile's periodic flooding in ancient times inspired the creation of scales to mark flood levels and calendars to identify harvest times. Today, we continue to use nature's rhythms and movements—the Earth's revolution around the sun, the weather, the temperature—to regulate and plan our activities.

In two-dimensional design, rhythm is the movement from one idea, compositional area, or element to another. It is the result of hierarchy, contrast, and structure, and involves timing and spacing (figure 5-16). In music, time is manipulated through the pacing of components. To create an understandable and engaging rhythm in visual form, the spacing or intervals among elements becomes an important consideration.

The series of page spreads in figure 5-18 are related by idea and held together by symmetry, while the sizes and colors of the elements change in accordance with the pacing of the text.

By its nature, rhythm also involves repetition and can lead to the formation of patterns. Throughout history, patterns have served as decorative elements and as a means of conveying tradition or power. Patterns are created by grouping a single element or repeating multiple elements (figures 5-19 and 5-20).

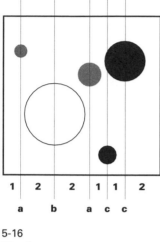

5-16
Rhythm

Rhythm can be created through the types of elements used (a, b, and c, each with a different value), their placement (1, 2), and at times, their association.

5-17
Bar Code

The spacing between the vertical lines of a bar code not only conveys pricing information but also creates a simple visual rhythm.

5-18
Pages from *Re-Thinking Design*, essay titled "Do Nothing," 1992
P. Scott Makela

The rhythm in layering among pages seeks to heighten the reading of a text that suggests the best design is often no design.

5-19
***Two Hundred Campbell's Soup Cans,* 1962**
Andy Warhol

Repetition can change or reveal the meaning of a single form. In this instance, a simple compositional method serves as a commentary on mass production and the icons of popular culture.

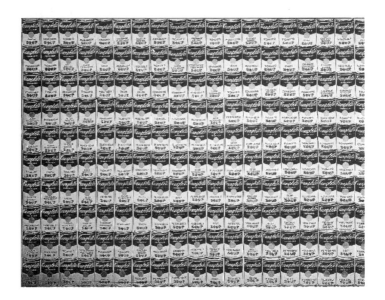

5-20
Blouse Pattern, Amuzgo, Guerrero, Mexico
Designer Unknown

Repetition of a given organization can create a larger pattern in which the single unit assumes a new appearance.

Ways of Creating Continuity

Structure

Structure refers to the internal parts of a form that support and define its appearance and contribute to conveying its message. Forms of all types have an underlying structure from those natural, such as the skeletal structure of our bodies to the internal framework of the buildings in the human-made environment. Structure holds components and ideas together, and is generally necessary to create meaning and a sense of continuity.

In a composition, structure can be revealed through elements, including those depicted literally, as in figure 5-22. The male figures create distinct triangles with their arms and legs, which contrasts with the stable vertical background and lamenting figures to the left. Taken together, this relationship heightens the work's symbolic meaning of men leaving for battle to the anguish of their loved ones.

Structure can also be revealed through the use of grids, which are (generally) evenly spaced vertical, horizontal, and/or diagonal lines (figure 5-21). The intersections of the lines result in quadrants where components can be aligned or placed in contrast. Grids are generally determined by the type, shape, size, and quantity of the corresponding material and are used extensively for organizing ideas and information. The simple, visible grid in figure 5-23 is both a visual element and a vehicle for creating hierarchy.

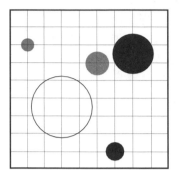

5-21
Structure

Grids provide a visual reference to a composition's organizational structure.

"Design is the conscious effort to impose meaningful order."[6]

Victor Papanek

5-22
Oath of the Horatii, **1785**
Jacques-Louis David

Structure can create order and heighten visual and conceptual relationships.

5-23
Poster for an Exhibition of Posters, 1980
Josef Mueller-Brockmann

Grids can structure information and create continuity among separate elements.

"The grid allows endless individual variations."[7]

Josef Mueller-Brockmann

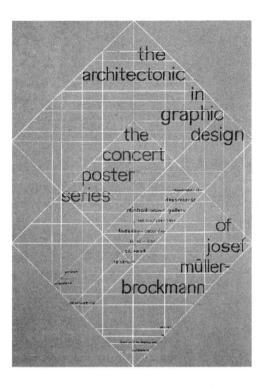

5-24
Map of Washington, D.C., 1887
Designer Unknown

In addition to organizing form, grids can have symbolic functions as well. Structure can further a sense of power and place value on elements. In this example, the primary buildings of the legislative, judicial, and executive branches are emphasized over other governmental buildings and the city at large.

Geometry and Ratios

The points, lines, and angles of geometry are useful tools for understanding the structure of natural and human-made forms. Geometry can simplify complex visual relationships and has long served as a descriptive device of our world. Through geometry, numerical ratios can be calculated and used to structure form.

Perhaps the best-known ratio is that found in the Fibonacci series. This group of whole numbers is named after the thirteenth-century Italian mathematician Leonardo Fibonacci who advocated it as evidence of a rational order in nature. The numerical relationships in the Fibonacci series define the structure of numerous natural forms, including the nautilus shell (figure 5-25). Such patterns illustrate that nature, on occasion, has logical, geometric, and numerically identifiable structures.

Each number in the Fibonacci series is the sum of the two previous numbers. Any number in the series divided by the following is approximately 0.618, and any number divided by the previous is approximately 1.618. This ratio is often called the *golden section* and underlies geometric shapes used throughout history.

5-25
Shell of the Nautilus Crab
Scott Camazine, Photographer

When compared numerically, the progressive compartments of the Nautilus shell exhibit the Fibonacci series.

1, 1, 2, 3, 5, 8, 13, 21 . . .
Fibonacci Series

5-26
Ratios of Common Shapes

Numbers can describe proportional relationships among parts of a form or parts of several forms.

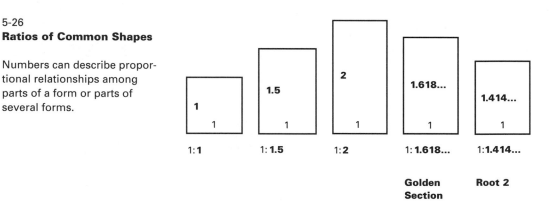

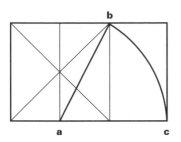

5-27
Golden Section
Ratio: 1:1.618 . . .

A square is divided to find the center point (a), from which length (a,b) is found. From point (a) the length is swung as an arc to point (c) to create a rectangle of golden section proportions.

5-28
Cherto Ketl, New Mexico, A.D. 1000
Russ Finley, Photographer

This prehistoric Pueblo Indian village housed more than 1,000 people in rooms of various sizes and shapes, most of which followed golden section proportions.[9]

The Golden Section

Perhaps the most historically significant use of geometry in the design of usable form is the *golden section* (also known as the *golden mean* or *golden rectangle*) (figure 5-27). The proportional relationship of the golden section has been applied both intentionally and unintentionally in two- and three-dimensional design. Notable intentional examples include the paintings of Barnett Newman, architecture of ancient Rome, and Cherto Ketl (figure 5-28), although in this instance it is unclear if the ratio was derived geometrically.

The golden section occurs in a variety of natural forms and is considered visually pleasing to a variety of cultures. However, some psychological studies suggest that, under controlled conditions, the rectangle is not preferred over other proportions.[8] Hence, while many common objects, such as credit cards and driver's licenses, approach golden section proportions, the question remains whether the golden section is pleasing in and of itself or pleasing because we are accustomed to its frequent use.

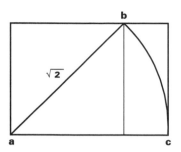

5-29
Root 2 Rectangle
Ratio: 1:1.414 . . .

From point (a) the length (a,b) is swung as an arc to point (c) to create a rectangle of root 2 proportions.

The Root 2 Rectangle

The root 2 rectangle is a proportional relationship similar to the golden section (figure 5-29). While the golden section has a longer recorded history and has been used extensively in two- and three-dimensional form, the root 2 is currently more relevant and is used primarily in two-dimensional form.

Andrea Palladio (Italian, 1508–1580) was the first person known to have applied root 2 proportions in interior design. More recently, root 2 proportions have been used in paper and envelope sizes in countries around the world (figure 5-30). This use grew out of a root 2–based system established in Germany in 1922, commonly referred to as DIN (Deutsches Institut für Normung).

A proportional standard for paper originates from the molds used in early European paper production. The root 2 rectangle can be divided or multiplied to yield additional root 2 rectangles, resulting in more economical paper manufacturing, storage, and printing.

5-30
Posters in the Streets of Switzerland, 1996

A related proportion can create a unified visual grouping and allow for better communication through easy identification.

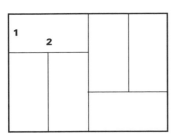

5-31
Tatami
1:2 Ratio

5-32
Interior Based on the Tatami

The Tatami mats positioned together with the divisions of sliding doorways create asymmetrical arrangments and emphasizes the movement from interior to exterior.

Tatami

Tatami straw floor mats, approximately 3 by 6 feet in length and 2 inches thick, are based on a rectangle of two squares (figure 5-31). The mats have been used for centuries in Japanese homes, where Tatami proportions also dictate the size and shape of the rooms (figure 5-32).

The Tatami rectangle can be divided or multiplied while maintaining constant visual unity. Its unity and efficient use of area reflect a culture where space is highly valued.

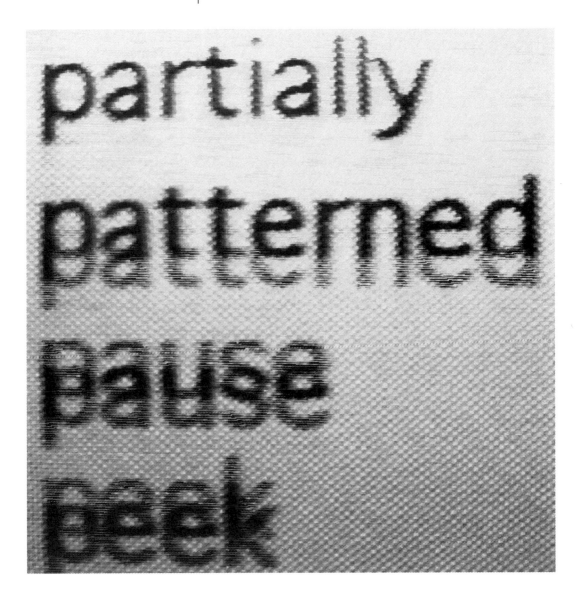

About This Chapter

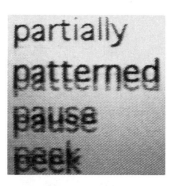

This chapter examines communication through symbols, letters, and images, whether in symbolic or metaphoric form. It addresses the responsibility of the designer in sending messages and the audience in receiving and interpreting them.

Concepts and Terms in This Chapter

Messages

Communication

Denotation/Connotation

Audience

Signals/Cues

Dissemination

Symbols/Alphabets

Imagery/Symbolism

Coding/Decoding

Metaphors

Propaganda/Persuasion

Responsibility/Voice

6-1 (Previous page and above)
***Alphabetically Sorted,* 1996
(Video Still)**
Rebeca Bollinger

Selected words beginning with each letter of the alphabet are scrolled to explore how words can be grouped and emphasized to reveal relationships and biases in the language of interactive on-line services.

Analyzing Messages

Focusing on Meaning

To create meaningful form, you must understand the ways and implications of sending, receiving, and interpreting messages.

Messages can be produced and interpreted through elements and color alone, or through symbols, letters, and photographic images. Individually or in combination, these connect the sender with the receiver and convey ideas, concepts, and information.

To critically send, receive, and interpret messages, you must be able to distinguish between what is meaningful and meaningless, useful and useless.

The word *communication* comes from the Latin word *communicare,* which means to make common. Communication involves a sender and a receiver, a message, a medium (such as a poster), and a shared understanding of basic elements, including words and symbols.

Communication is a science, as evidenced by research and theory that explores the processes involved. It is also a creative act in that a given message can be sent or interpreted differently. When we communicate, we cannot be certain that the message of a sign is understood, especially when communicating to persons from other cultures. We each have our own biases, experiences, and knowledge that influence how we process and act upon messages.

Basis and Types of Messages

Communication

Producing and interpreting messages in visual form can be immediately understandable or deliberately ambiguous (figure 6-3). Either way, a message can have many layers of meaning and be directed to specific or wide-ranging audiences who determine its clarity or ambiguity. To aid this process, particularly when clarity is desired, visual guides in the form of signals and cues become useful components to guiding interpretation and understanding function (figures 6-2 and 6-4).

As seen throughout this book, components used to send messages denote and connote meaning. For example, while a square denotes a shape of four equal sides, it may connote stability or neutrality, and has even been identified as the shape that embodies the color red.[2] The extent to which such associations and connotations are universally assigned and understood is open to debate.

Messages can be designed from a range of theoretical viewpoints. The more dominant viewpoint and basis for this book is termed *motivational design:* identifying needs and creating forms to serve those needs. Stimulus-response design is another approach and is more specific to graphic design and advertising. Although it can meet needs, it can also create them. It is based on repeatedly exposing an audience to a sign, such as a company symbol, to establish a connection between stimulus (exposure to the symbol) and response (purchase or other action).

6-2
Signaling

Signals can help the audience better understand a message's meaning. In common software interface design, a change in value typically signals the results of an action.

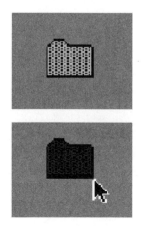

6-3
**Poster for an Academic
Fiber Program, 1984**
Jeff Keedy

Images, words, and symbols
can express deeper meanings
than is possible through literal
depiction.

The designer of this work takes
issue with the prevalence of
transmitting unambiguous
information and called this
work "an exercise in doing
everything wrong."[3]

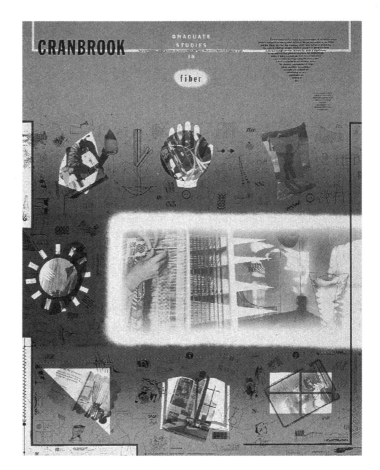

6-4
Cues

The use and meaning of forms
can be clarified or clouded by
accompanying visual and verbal cues. The word *push* on this
door is in contradiction to the
design and use of the handle.

Implications of Conveying Messages

Dissemination

Dissemination refers to sending messages generally on a wide scale, and is common in applied design activity. Whether broadly distributed or presented in a more intimate scale such as an exhibition space, the method, length, and location messages are sent and received influences their appearance, interpretation, and resulting response.

Throughout this book, a number of factors have been examined that influence dissemination, including societal attitudes, philosophical thought, and target audience. From the use of inscriptions on architecture throughout history to more portable forms, the physical form and location and the technology employed in the creation and transmission of a message play significant roles in its usefulness, meaning, and impact.

Advances in printing in the mid-fifteenth century in Korea and in Europe by Johannes Gutenberg (1387–1468) allowed for faster, less expensive duplication of written messages (figure 6-5). This resulted in more accurate written information available to more of the population.

Current technologies, including television and the Internet, have shaped design (figure 6-6) and furthered dissemination of information (and misinformation) by allowing relatively easy and rapid access and interaction on a global scale. This has broadened our sense of place and altered our identity as we create and interact in communities that are no longer identified by traditional physical locations. Individual choice has also been heightened and traditional linear reading conventions supplanted, as information in digital environments is often presented in layers to be accessed in any order.

"Societies have always been shaped more by the nature of the media by which men communicate than by the content of the communication."[4]

Marshall McLuhan and Quentin Fiore

6-5
Bible, 1457
Johannes Gutenberg

The Gutenberg Bible is among the first known results of movable type, a process that greatly accelerated the dissemination of information. The letters shown, designed to resemble hand-drawn letters printing replaced, were common at the time and considered readable.

6-6
MTVPE, 1997
(Font Design for MTV)
PlazmMedia
Joshua Berger, Niko Courtelis,
Art Directors and Designers;
Pete McCracken, Art Director
and Principal Font Designer;
Riq Mosqueda, Designer

The extreme contrast in form
(smooth edges against right
angles) and dynamic tension
(note the letter s), is suggestive
of the target audience. The simplicity is directed toward it's
use (short words and number
combinations) and context (for
viewing on predominately low
resolution television screens).

ABCDEFGHIJ
KLMNOPQRST
UVWXYZ
abcdefghij
klmnopqrst
uvwxyz
123456789

Mtype

6-7
MTVPE, 1997
PlazmMedia

The design and use of a font
not only carry messages but
become part of the message.

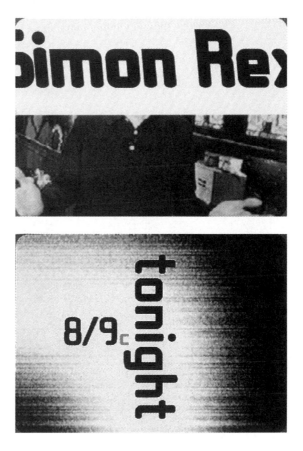

Ways of Conveying Messages

Symbols, Alphabets, and Writing

Symbols and alphabets are codes that allow the transmission and understanding of complex messages (figure 6-9). They are the foundation of writing, which is a sign system that represents speech. These have evolved over thousands of years and continue to do so in response to social, cultural, philosophical, and technological changes.

Early humans communicated through pictographs (figure 6-10); from these came more complex pictographs and early writing systems (figure 6-11). Some of these systems contained up to 2,000 symbols that, when combined, communicated ideas and aided recall. Ideograms evolved primarily in China about the same time (figure 6-12). These are symbols that stand for an idea but are not phonetic representations of spoken language. Ideograms are still in use today by an estimated one-fifth of the world's population and in numerous Eastern languages, some of which use over 40,000 characters.

The transition from pictographs and early writing systems to the alphabet remains unknown. The first alphabet (named for the first two letters of the Greek alphabet, *alpha* and *beta*) is believed to be Phoenician in origin (1500–700 B.C.) This eventually developed into the Roman alphabet, around the sixth century B.C. Alphabetic systems use a limited number of symbols representing individual spoken sounds (figure 6-13).

6-8
Graffiti

Symbols and writing can serve as identifiers of the sender and, in this example, mark territory.

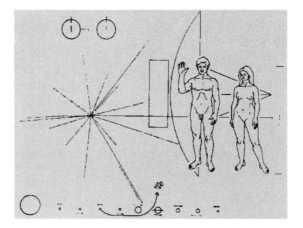

6-9
Plaque Aboard Pioneer 10, Launched July 4, 1976
NASA

Symbols signifying the Earth's basic elements, and its position in the solar system and the origin of Pioneer 10 are included in this plaque. The male and female figures are generalized (questionably) to represent humankind. The male's hand is raised in a gesture of goodwill.

6-10
**Cave Marking,
15,000–10,000 B.C.**
Lascaux, France
Early Pictograph

Cave drawings communicated
information and aided in the
search for meaning.

6-11
Clay Tablet, 3000 B.C.
Damascus, Syria
Pictograph

A wedge-shaped tool was used
to press markings into clay.
This tablet tracked the number
of animals assigned to civil
servants.

6-12
Colophon, 1370
Yang Wei-chen
Ideogram

Common to eastern calligra-
phy, this work includes a series
of seals (on the far right)
printed from porcelain blocks
that identify the maker.

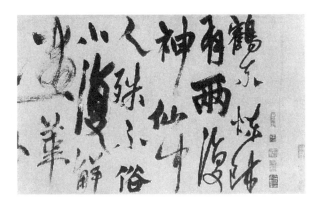

6-13
Bodoni, Late 1700's
Giambattista Bodoni
Alphabet

Often called the first modern
font, the stark geometry of
Bodoni departs from earlier
printed forms that retain hand-
drawn qualities (figure 6-5).

ABCDEFGHIJKLMNOPQRSTUVWXYZ
abcdefghijklmnopqrstuvwxyz

Imagery and Symbolism

Imagery in the broadest sense includes that which is created with basic components such as shape and color, as well as symbols, letters, and images photographic in origin. The latter of these, depending on their manipulation and use, can create a more direct presentation of an issue or concept beyond what is possible through other means. Such images often contain more familiar and/or culturally meaningful objects or signs that enhance the ability for more immediate and targeted responses.

To further response recognizable parts or readily evident themes may be taken (*appropriated*) from other images or cultural contexts and put to new use (figure 6-14). Such practice can raise legal questions of ownership (the majority of images appearing in the public domain are copyrighted) and ethical concerns of appropriateness particularly when sacred religious objects or those symbolic of a nation are used.

Symbolism describes using components, objects and images as coded symbols to express intangible, complex, or multiple meanings. Coded symbols are learned or understood through decoding—analysis and interpretation that examines presentations in relation to the context, purpose, and audience a message (figure 6-15).

6-14
Advertisement, 1996
Wieden and Kennedy
Eugene Richards, Photographer

Imagery may create identities and target specific audiences by using commonly held perceptions, such as the cowboy as rugged and adventuresome.

6-15
Airport: Cat Paws, 1974
Robert Rauschenberg

Work may contain overt or obscure signifiers (elements that create, or point to, coded meaning) that when decoded reveal additional understandings, including those religious and sexual in nature, common in Rauschenberg's work.

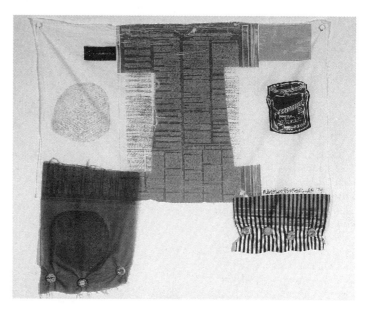

6-16
The Kitchen Knife Cuts Through the Weimar Beer-Belly Culture, 1919
Hannah Höch

The juxtaposition of images express chaos and corruption in this example from the Dada movement.

6-17
The Gates in Bellinzona, from *Projects*, 1978
Gregory Vines, Designer
Wolfgang Weingart, Editor

The gates in southern Switzerland serve as a segue into the people, culture, and history of a region. Represented through a variety of means, the gate form allows for layers of associations and connotations.

Metaphors

A metaphor is a way of revealing deeper meaning and under-standing of complex or abstract concepts (figure 6-18).

In the broadest sense, all visual forms in two-dimensional de-sign might be thought of as metaphors because they represent ideas, concerns, and/or physical objects. Some shapes or colors can take on meaning beyond their primary or literal appear-ance (figure 6-21). Whether abstract or literal, the elements carry references to other events or meanings that can enrich the message.

Aristotle said that a good metaphor implies an intuitive per-ception of the similarity between dissimilar things.[5] Using a metaphor is to give meaning to a subject by using a visual image that is not inherently a part of that subject.

6-18
Calla Leaves, **1929**
Imogen Cunningham

Natural forms serve as a metaphor for sensual growth and discovery.

6-19
IBM Rebus, **1980**
Paul Rand

A metaphor can take the form
of a pun, as in this example
where the letters of the IBM
logo are playfully recreated
in pictorial form.

6-20
IBM Logo, 1956
Paul Rand

6-21
Rothko Chapel, 1971
Mark Rothko (Paintings,
1965–66)
Philip Johnson, Architect

Repeated color, texture, and
shape in concert with their
physical context are used as a
metaphorical symbol to
heighten the experience of con-
templation and exchange.

The Use of Messages

Propaganda and Persuasion

Propaganda and persuasion activities are related and even identical, depending on your point of view.

Propaganda presents information or relationships for the purpose of gaining or maintaining power and control. It may offer a distorted view of reality and of generally accepted truths but, as with all messages, depends on interpretation and point of view. Propaganda takes many forms and is particularly prevalent during war and elections to stir emotions and call people to action (figure 6-22).

Persuasion encourages people to reconsider their attitudes, engage in self-reflection, or take an action such as purchasing a product or service. Persuasion can also inform and enlighten, and thus is not necessarily a negative activity.

Persuasive messages can be personal, open-ended, and viewed in an intimate environment or dispersed to a broad audience in the form of advertising. In its best form, persuasive advertising can raise awareness as well as sell a product (figure 6-23). In its worst form, it simply encourages us to consume without regard to actual need, impact on the environment, or our collective quality of life.

6-22
Nazi Propaganda Map, 1939

Nazi propaganda used maps to distort and sway public opinion. By altering the tonal values used to depict countries, Germany misrepresented their alliances and appeared to be gaining the support of its neighbors.

6-23
**Advertisement for United
Colors of Benetton, 1992**
Concept: O. Toscani
United Colors of Benetton

By focusing on the human con-
sequences of a natural disaster,
conflict, and human tragedy,
the advertiser increases public
awareness and indirectly per-
suades the audience to purchase the company's clothing.

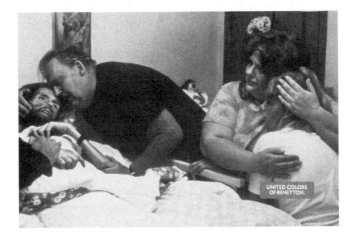

A Further Perspective

Responsibility and Voice

We are responsible for the ways we address issues and transmit ideas, concerns, and information. While there are few guidelines for acting responsibly, continued growth, critical self-reflection, and openness to others can nourish the process. Acting responsibly includes considering your client (if involved) and audience, the subject matter addressed, the portrayal of others, and the environmental effects of the materials you use.

Because much of design is based on solving external problems, designers often address concerns, ideas, and information that lie outside their experience or view of the world. However, this does not prevent designers from expressing personal concerns when appropriate for the audience and client. However, the need for self-expression and asserting one's own agenda must often be balanced with the responsibility to consider alternative points of view and the needs of others.

As you create and send messages, you develop your own voice, which is a combination of experience, skill, concern, desire, and spirit. Developing your own voice through critical examination of all you do can enrich your experience and work. Asserting your voice, when appropriate, can further your contribution to others. This can be done through the use of a particular visual component, methodology, the work you choose to engage in, and the issues you address.

While we are united by the common experience of humanity, we each have individual experiences, interests, and abilities that make us unique. Drawing on these as well as learning, research, and outside input can result in work that is original and meaningful to ourselves and others.

6-24

Front and back covers from
The Portrait Series, 1996
Warren Lehrer

This portrayal of body types, clothing, and postures seeks to comment on individual and group identities. This is illustrated by each figure looking toward and away, the group seen from front and back, and individuals enclosed in common yet separate spaces.

6-25

Suit #2, 1996
David Dunlap

The relationship among message, sender and receiver are examined in this work that celebrates the dream of Dr. Martin Luther King. Written and visual interpretations of King's life become symbolic of shared concerns.

Endnotes

Introduction

1
James O. Freedman, *Idealism and Liberal Education* (Ann Arbor: The University of Michigan Press, 1996), 2.

Chapter 1

1
American Center for Design, *American Center for Design* (Chicago: American Center for Design, 1994).

2
Max Bill and Ettore Sottsass, Jr. "Design and Theory: Two Points of View" in *Design Since 1945,* ed. Kathryn B. Hiesinger (Philadelphia: The Philadelphia Museum of Art, 1983), 3.

3
Meredith Davis and Robin Moore, *Education Through Design: Middle School Curriculum* (Raleigh: North Carolina State University and North Carolina Arts Council, 1993).

4
Norman Potter, *What Is a Designer: Things, Places, Messages* (London: Hyphen Press, 1980), 13.

5
Quote used with permission of Massimo Vignelli.

6
Horatio Greenough, *The Travels, Observations, and Experiences of a Yankee Stonecutter* (New York: G. P. Putnam), 1852.

7
Peter Blake, *Form Follows Fiasco: Why Modern Architecture Hasn't Worked* (Boston and Toronto: Little, Brown, 1977).

8
Sharon Wood, "He's Got a Thing for Bridges," *Oregonian,* Monday, 24 June 1996, p. C1.

9
Andrea Branzi, *Learning from Milan* (Cambridge: MIT Press, 1988), 32.

10
Daniel Boorstin, *The Discoverers* (New York: Vintage Press, 1983), 98.

11
Dieter Rams, quoted from a lecture at the Ninth Annual Design Management Conference, Martha's Vineyard, Massachusetts, June 1979. Quote used with permission of the Design Management Conference.

12

George Nelson, "The Design Process," *Design Since 1945,* ed. Kathryn B. Hiesinger (Philadelphia: The Philadelphia Museum of Art, 1983), 10.

13

"An Interview with Lucille Tenazas," *Statements* 6, no. 2 (Winter 1991; Chicago: American Center for Design): 16–17.

14

Meredith Davis and Robin Moore, *Education Through Design: Middle School Curriculum* (Raleigh: North Carolina State University and North Carolina Arts Council, 1993), 19.

Chapter 2

1

Paul Rand, "Observations on Intuition," *STA Journal* (1987): 68–69.

2

Quote used with permission of Dr. Allan Sandage, Carnegie Observatory, Pasadena, California.

3

Rudolf Arnheim, "Gestalt Psychology and Artistic Form," in *Aspects of Form* (Bloomington: Indiana University Press), 1966, 204–205.

4

Richard Saul Wurman, *Information Anxiety* (New York: Doubleday, 1991), 42–45, 59–61.

5

James L. Harrison, *Typography* (Washington, D.C.: Government Printing Office, 1951), 14.

6

Mario Bellini, quoted from a lecture given at the International Design Conference at Aspen, Aspen, Colorado, June 1989. Quote used with permission of Mario Bellini and the International Design Conference at Aspen.

Chapter 4

1

Johannes Itten, *The Elements of Color* (New York: Van Nostrand Reinhold, 1970), 61.

2

Josef Albers, *The Interaction of Color* (New Haven, Conn.: Yale University Press, 1963), 5.

3

Deborah Sharpe, *The Psychology of Color and Design* (Totowa, N.J.: Littlefield, Adams, 1975), 9, 14, 18–19.

4

Information provided by the Gay and Lesbian Historical Society of Northern California, San Francisco, California.

Chapter 5

1

Arthur Drexler, *Ludwig Mies van der Rohe* (New York: George Braziller, 1960), 31.

2

Robert Venturi, *Complexity and Contradiction in Architecture* (New York: Museum of Modern Art, 1967), 17.

3

George Johnson, "Researchers on Complexity Ponder What It's All About" *New York Times,* Tuesday, 6 May 1997, p. B9.

4

Gyorgy Kepes, *The Language of Vision* (Chicago: Paul Theobald, 1969), 36.

5

Alfred L. Yarbus, *Eye Movements and Vision* (New York: Plenum Press, 1967), 190.

6

Victor Papanek, *Design for The Real World* (Chicago: Academic Publishers, Chicago, 1972), 17.

7

Yvonne Schwemer-Scheddin, "Interview with Josef Mueller-Brockmann," *Eye,* (Winter 1995): 14.

8

I. C. McManus, "The Aesthetics of Simple Figures," *British Journal of Psychology* 71 (1980): 505–524.

9

Alden C. Hayes, David M. Brugge, and W. James Judge, *Archeological Surveys of Chaco Canyon, New Mexico* (Washington, D.C.: National Park Service, United States Department of the Interior, 1981), 60–61.

Chapter 6

1

Werner J. Severin and James W. Tankard, Jr., *Communication Theories: Origins, Methods and Uses* (New York: Hastings House Publishers, 1970), 6.

2

Johannes Itten, *The Elements of Color* (New York: Van Nostrand Reinhold, 1970), 75.

3

Rick Poynor, "Remove Specifics and Convert to Ambiguities" *Eye* 5, no. 20 (Spring 1996): 64.

4

Marshall McLuhan, and Quentin Fiore, *The Medium Is the Massage* (New York: Bantam Books, 1967), 8.

5

Aristotle, *The Poetics* (Cambridge: Harvard University Press, 1995), 105.

6

Peter Selz, *Mark Rothko* (New York: Arno Press for The Museum of Modern Art, 1972), 9.

7

Chuck Carlson, Tim Hartford, and Carl Wohlt, *The Graphic Design Handbook for Business* (Chicago: AIGA, Chicago 1995), 12.

8

Garland Kirkpatrick, "A Noticeable Absence," *Sphere* 1, no. 1: 10.

9

David Dunlap, *This Is Always Finished* (Des Moines, Iowa: Des Moines Art Center, 1989), 6.

Bibliography

In addition to those sources cited in the endnotes, the following were consulted in the writing of this book. The list represents only some of the many that have been influential to me, these are given as sources for you to explore.

Form, Structure, and Color

Berger, John. *Ways of Seeing.* New York: Viking Press, 1972.

Dondis, Donis. *A Primer of Visual Literacy.* Cambridge: MIT Press, 1973.

Hofmann, Armin. *Graphic Design Manual.* New York: Van Nostrand Reinhold, 1965.

Maier, Manfred. *Basic Principles of Design.* New York: Van Nostrand Reinhold, 1977.

Pile, John. *Design.* Amherst: The University of Massachusetts Press, 1979.

Rand, Paul. *A Designer's Art.* New Haven: Yale University Press, 1985.

Wong, Wucius. *Two-Dimensional Design.* New York: Van Nostrand Reinhold, 1972.

The Alphabet, Letterforms, and Symbols

Anderson, Donald M. *The Art of Written Forms.* New York: Holt, Rinehart and Winston, 1969.

Croy, Peter. *Symbols and Their Message.* Gottingen, Frankfurt, Zurich: Musterschmidt, 1972.

Gurtler, Andre. *The Development of the Roman Alphabet.* Basle: Bildungsverband Schweizerischer Buchdrucker, 1967.

Jung, Carl. *Man and His Symbols.* Garden City, N.Y.: Doubleday, 1964.

McLean, Ruari. *Typography.* New York: Thames and Hudson, 1980.

Speikermann, Erik. *Stop Stealing Sheep.* Mountain View, California: Adobe Press, 1993.

Steinberg, Sigfrid H. *Five Hundred Years of Printing.* London: Faber, 1959.

Sutton, James, and Alan Bartram. *An Atlas of Typeforms.* London: Lund and Humphries, 1968.

Criticism, History, and Related Theory

Adams, Hazard, and Leroy Seale. *Critical Theory Since 1965.* Tallahassee: Florida State University Press, 1986.

Barthes, Roland. *Mythologies.* New York: Noonday Press, 1972.

Birkets, Sven. *The Gutenberg Elegies.* Winchester, Massachusetts: Faber and Faber, 1994.

Buchanan, Richard, and Victor Margolin, eds. *Discovering Design.* Chicago: University of Chicago Press, 1995.

Burke, James. *The Day the Universe Changed.* Boston: Little, Brown, 1985.

Derrida, Jacques. *Of Grammatology.* Baltimore: Johns Hopkins University Press, 1976.

Doordan, Dennis P. *Design History: An Anthology.* Cambridge: MIT Press, 1995.

Eagleton, Terry. *Literary Theory: An Introduction.* Minneapolis: University of Minnesota Press, 1983.

Janson, H. W. *History of Art.* New York: Abrams, 1997.

Krauss, Rosalind E. *The Originality of the Avant-Garde and Other Modernist Myths.* Cambridge: MIT Press, 1985.

Lechte, John. *Fifty Key Contemporary Thinkers: From Structuralism to Postmodernity.* London and New York: Routledge, 1994.

Lupton, Ellen, and J. Abbott Miller. *Design, Writing, Research.* New York: Kiosk, 1996.

Margolin, Victor, ed. *Design Discourse: History, Theory, Criticism.* Chicago: University of Chicago Press, 1989.

Meggs, Philip. *A History of Graphic Design.* New York: John Wiley & Sons, 1997.

Muller-Brockmann, Josef. *History of Visual Communication.* New York: Hastings House, 1971.

Sparke, Penny. *An Introduction to Design and Culture in the Twentieth Century.* London: Allen and Unwin, 1986.

Toffler, Alvin. *Future Shock.* New York: Random House, 1970.

Tansey, Richard G., and Fred S. Kleiner. *Gardner's Art Through the Ages.* Fort Worth, Texas: Harcourt Brace College Publishers, 1996.

Walker, John. *Design History and the History of Design.* London: Pluto Press, 1989.

Methods, Research, and Related Theory

Arnheim, Rudolf. *Art and Visual Perception: A Psychology of the Creative Eye.* Berkeley: University of California Press, 1974.

Bloomer, Carolyn. *Principles of Visual Perception.* New York: Van Nostrand Reinhold, 1976.

Crozier, Ray. *Manufactured Pleasures: Psychological Responses to Design.* Manchester and New York: Manchester University Press, 1994.

Doyle, Charlotte. *Explorations in Psychology.* Monterey, Calif.: Brooks and Cole, 1987.

Forty, Adrian. *Objects of Desire: Design and Society 1750–1980.* London: Thames and Hudson, 1986.

Held, Richard, comp. *Scientific American: Image, Object, and Illusion.* San Francisco: W. H. Freeman, 1971.

Minsky, Marvin. *The Society of Mind.* New York: Simon and Shuster, 1986.

Norman, Donald. *Psychology of Everyday Things.* New York: Basic Books, 1988.

Petroski, Henry. *The Evolution of Useful Things.* New York: Vintage Books, 1992.

Scholfield, P.H. *The Theory of Proportion in Architecture.* Cambridge: Cambridge University Press, 1958.

Tufte, Edward R. *The Visual Display of Quantitative Information.* Cheshire, Conn.: Graphics Press, 1983.

Woolsey, Kristina Hooper. *VizAbility.* Boston: PWS Publishing, 1996.

Image Credits

Introduction

0-1
Image and Permission: Frank Gehry and Associates
0-2
Image: American Foundation for Aids Research; Permission: AmFAR and Ken Freidman

Chapter 1

1-1
Author
1-2
Author
1-3
Image and Permission: Professor Guillermo Algaze, University of California, San Diego
1-4
Author
1-5
Image and Permission: Gallaudet University Press
1-6
Image: Nimatallah/Art Resource, NY; Permission: Art Resource and (C) Artists Rights Society (ARS), New York/ADAGP, Paris
1-7
Image and Permission: The Nelson-Atkins Museum of Art, Kansas City, Missouri (Purchase: Nelson Trust)
1-8
Image and Permission: Douglas Mazonowicz/Art Resource, NY
1-9
Image and Permission: Harper Collins Publishers, Copyright 1994
1-10
Image and Permission: Courtesy of George Eastman House
1-11
Image and Permission: Jessie Levine, Copyright 1982, 1990 (415) 494-7729
1-12
Image and Permission: Division of Tourism/Worlds' Only Corn Palace
1-13
Author

Chapter 2

2-1
Author
2-2
Image and Permission: Imperial War Museum, London
2-3
Author
2-4
Image and Permission: Mrs. Marion S. Rand
2-5–2-9
Author
2-10, 2-11
Image and Permission: Courtesy of American Institute of Graphic Arts. From *Symbol Signs,* second edition (New York: AIGA, 1993). Reprinted with permission
2-12
Author
2-13
Image and Permission: Pacific Bell
2-14
Image and Permission: Morningstar
2-15
Image and Permission: London Transit Museum
2-16
Image and Permission: Renee Crago Fisher
2-17, 2-18
Author
2-19–2-21
Images and Permission: Joy Panos Stauber and Collective Incorporated

Chapter 3

3-1
Image and Permission: Copyright Inter IKEA Systems BV 1997, Reprinted with permission of Inter IKEA Systems BV
3-2
Author
3-3
Image and Permission: Courtesy of Hunt Institute for Botanical Documentation, Carnegie-Mellon University, Pittsburgh, Pennsylvania
3-4
Image: Art Resource, NY; Permission: Art Resource, (C) 1998 Estate of Pablo Picasso/Artists Rights Society (ARS) New York
3-5
Image and Permission: Michael Bowers
3-6, 3-7
Author
3-8–3-10
Images and Permission: Michelle Oka Doner
3-11–3-14
Author
3-15
Image: Portland Art Museum Permission: Portland Art Museum and Pace-Widenstein Gallery, New York

3-16
Image and Permission: Kevin Donahue
3-17
Image and Permission: Courtesy of the Artist and Klein Art Works, Chicago
3-18–3-20
Author
3-21
Image: Reinhold Brown Gallery, NY; Permission: Reinhold Brown Gallery, NY and (C) 1998 Artists Rights Society (ARS), New York/ ADAGP, Paris
3-22
Image and Permission: Allgemeine Plakatgesellschaft
3-23
Permission: Nike, Inc.
3-24
Image: University of Iowa Museum of Art, Gift of Peggy Guggenheim, Copyright 1959; Permission: University of Iowa Museum of Art and (C) 1998 Pollock-Krasner Foundation/Artists Rights Society (ARS), New York
3-25–3-28
Author
3-29
Image and Permission: Johnson and Wolverton
3-30
Image and Permission: Library of Congress
3-31
Author
3-32
Image and Permission: Walker Art Center and Matt Eller
3-33
Image: National Gallery of Art; Permission: Ailsa Mellon Bruce Fund (C) 1997 Board of Trustees, National Gallery of Art, Washington and (C) 1998 Succession H. Matisse, Paris/Artists Rights Society (ARS), New York
3-34
Image and Permission: Chermayeff and Geismar
3-35
Author
3-36
Image and Permission: Oregon State University Extension Service
3-37
Image and Permission: Erich Lessing/Art Resource, NY
3-38
Image and Permission: Portland Art Museum
3-39
Image and Permission: Lisa Strausfeld, Copyright of Massachusetts Institute of Technology, 1994
3-40
Author
3-41
Image and Permission: The Metropolitan Museum of Art
3-42
Image and Permission: Copyright (c) 1944 (Renewed) by G. Schirmer, Inc. (ASCAP) International Copyright Secured. All Rights Reserved. Reprinted by Permission.

3-43

Image: Giraudon/Art Resource, NY, Permission: Art Resource, NY and (C) Mondrian Estate/Holtzman Trust

Chapter 4

4-1, 4-2
Images and Permission: Wolfgang Weingart
4-3–4-5
Author
4-6
Image and Permission: Wolfgang Weingart
4-7
Image and Permission: Photograph (C) 1996, The Art Institute of Chicago, Helen Birch Bartlett Memorial Collection
4-8
Author
4-9
Image and Permission: The Pierpont Morgan Library/Art Resource, NY
4-10, 4-11
Author
4-12
Image and Permission: Portland Art Museum
4-13–4-16
Author
4-17
Image: Portland Art Museum, Permission: Portland Art Museum, (C) 1998 The Josef and Anni Albers Foundation/Artists Rights Society (ARS), New York
4-18
Image and Permission: Armin Hofmann
4-19
Author
4-20
Image and Permission: Copyright, Woodmansterne, United Kingdom
4-21
Author
4-22
Image and Permission: Lucille Tenazas
4-23
Image and Permission: Sussman/Prejza and Company, Inc.
4-24
Image: Art Resource, NY, Permission: Art Resource, NY and the Estate of Renate Hoffman
4-25
Image and Permission: Gay and Lesbian Historical Society of Northern California

Chapter 5

5-1
Image and Permission: America Hurrah Archive, NYC
5-2
Permission: Thomas Ockerse

5-3
Permission: April Greiman and "Stamp Design (C) 1995 U.S. Postal Service, Reproduced with permission."
5-4
Author
5-5
Image and Permission: Henry Dreyfuss and Associates, and Watson-Guptill
5-6
Image: Giraudon/Art Resource, NY; Permission: Art Resource, NY and the Egyptian Museum, Cairo
5-7
Image and Permission: Alinari/Art Resource, NY
5-8
Author
5-9
Image and Permission: Plenum Publishing Corporation
5-10
Image and Permission: Mauricio Lasansky, The Lasansky Corporation
5-11
Image and Permission: Emigre
5-12
Author
5-13
Image and Permission: David Carson
5-14
Image and Permission: Verlag Niggli, AG
5-15
Image and Permission: Amon Carter Museum, Fort Worth, Texas; Laura Gilpin, The Church at Picuris Pueblo, New Mexico, 1963, Black and White Photograph, P19179.95.93
5-16
Author
5-17
Image and Permission: Bayer Corporation
5-18
Image: Mohawk Paper Company, Permission: P. Scott Makela
5-19
Image and Permission: Schalkwijk/Art Resource, NY, (C) 1998 Andy Warhol Foundation for the Visual Arts/Artists Rights Society (ARS), New York
5-20
Image and Permission: Art Resource, NY
5-21
Author
5-22
Image and Permission: Art Resource
5-23
Image and Permission: Reinhold Brown Gallery, NYC
5-24
Image and Permission: Library of Congress
5-25
Image and Permission: Photo Researchers, Inc., and (C) Scott Camazine, Photographer

5-26, 5-27
Author
5-28
Image: National Park Services, Permission: (C) 1984 Russ Findley
Photography
5-29
Author
5-30
Image and Permission: Allgemeine Plakatgesellschaft
5-31
Author
5-32
Image and Permission: Warner Blaser

Chapter 6

6-1
Image and Permission: Rebeca Bollinger
6-2
Author
6-3
Image and Permission: Jeff Keedy
6-4
Author
6-5
Image and Permission: The Pierpont Morgan Library/Art Resource,
NY
6-6, 6-7
Images and Permission: PlazmMedia
6-8
Author
6-9
Image and Permission: NASA
6-10
Image and Permission: Douglas Mazonowicz/Art Resource, NY
6-11
Image and Permission: Photo Researchers, Inc., (C) Gianni Tortoli,
Photographer
6-12
Image and Permission: Freer Gallery of Art, Smithsonian Institution
6-13
Adobe Font
6-14
Image and Permission: Wieden and Kennedy, Permission: Miller
Brewing Company and Eugene Richards
6-15
Image: Portland Art Museum, Vivian and Gordon Gilkey Graphic Arts
Collection, Permission: Portland Art Museum and (C) Robert
Rauschenberg/Licensed by VAGA, New York, NY, Published by
Graphicstudio, USF, Tampa, Florida
6-16
Image: Erich Lessing/Art Resource, NY, Permission: Erich
Lessing/Art Resource, NY, and (C) 1998 Artists Rights Society (ARS),
New York
6-17
Permission: Gregory Vines

6-18
Image and Permission: Photograph by Imogen Cunningham,
Copyright 1978 The Imogen Cunningham Trust
6-19
Permission: Mrs. Marion S. Rand, Permission: Mrs. Marion S. Rand
and IBM, IBM and the IBM logotype are registered trademarks of
International Business Machines Corporation
6-20
Image and Permission: IBM, IBM and the IBM logotype are
registered trademarks of International Business Machines
Corporation
6-21
Image: Rothko Foundation, Rothko Chapel, Permission: Rothko
Foundation, Rothko Chapel and (C) 1998 Kate Rothko-Prizel and
Christopher Rothko/Artists Rights Society (ARS), New York
6-22
Image and Permission: Cornell University Library
6-23
Images and Permission: Concept: O. Toscani, Courtesy of United
Colors of Benetton
6-24
Images and Permission: Warren Lehrer
6-25
Image and Permission: Rex Bavousett, University of Iowa, (C)
University Relations Publications, David Dunlap

Index